AN ENEMY AMONG FRIENDS

AN ENEMY AMONG FRIENDS

KIYOAKI MURATA

KODANSHA INTERNATIONAL
Tokyo • New York • London

Distributed in the United States by Kodansha America, Inc., 114 Fifth Avenue, New York, N.Y. 10011, and in the United Kingdom and continental Europe by Kodansha Europe Ltd., Gillingham House, 38-44 Gillingham Street, London SW1V 1HU. Published by Kodansha International Ltd., 17-14 Otowa 1-chome, Bunkyo-ku, Tokyo 112, and Kodansha America, Inc.

91 92 93 10 9 8 7 6 5 4 3 2 1

ISBN 4-7700-01609-3

Library of Congress Cataloging-in-Publication Data
Murata, Kiyoaki, 1922-
An enemy among friends / by Kiyoaki Murata.—1st ed.
    p.   cm.
ISBN 4-7700-1609-3:
1. Murata, Kiyoaki, 1922-. 2. World War, 1939-1945—
United States. 3. Japanese—United States—Biography.
4. Students—United States—Biography. 5.
Intellectuals—Japan—Biography. I. Title.
D769.8.A6M87 1991
973'.0495602—dc20
[B]
                                              91-4946
                                                  CIP

Contents

Preface 7

Prologue 11

1. Dreaming of America 14
2. First Impressions 25
3. The Darkening Skies 35
4. Struggle with English 40
5. St. Francis Wood 47
6. The Surprise Attack 56
7. Goodbye, Drew School 71
8. Visalia 88
9. Poston 109
10. Chicago 133
11. College at Last 146
12. My Longest Day 163
13. Carleton 178
14. "WAR IS OVER" 193
15. Chicago Again 210
16. The Long Wait 223
17. A Man with No Name 231

Epilogue 239

Preface

You are about to read an account of a young Japanese who arrived in the United States as a student on the eve of the Pacific War, and stayed there throughout and beyond the war years. This preface is intended to forewarn contemporary American readers about something they will not find here, whose absence they may find disconcerting.

The missing element is racial discrimination against the protagonist. If you expect these memoirs to be made up of a litany of outbursts of grief and fury by a victim of prejudice, you will be disappointed.

Yet you cannot be blamed if such are your expectations. The setting seems to have been perfect: In the first place I was a Japanese, a foreigner in America. In addition, I was officially an enemy alien, because of the unusual circumstances in which I found myself. The Pearl Harbor attack exposed Japan and Japanese people to violent opprobrium: They were characterized in the press as treacherous, cunning, untrustworthy, barbaric, bestial, sadistic, and so on, almost ad infinitum. Americans today over fifty years of age perhaps remember the intense anti-Japanese sentiment that enveloped continental America at that time. By today's standards, it would seem, I was doubly qualified to be a target of hatred. Yet such was not the case.

The fact is that I spent seven delightful and fruitful years in

America, including the war years, and found myself among friends wherever I went.

If this experience sounds incredible, I might offer some explanations, starting with my own psyche. I received a highly ethnocentric and nationalistic education in primary and secondary schools in Japan during the 1930s, and up to the early part of 1941, when I left home. We students were taught that Japan was superior to all other nations, and that we were fortunate to have been born Japanese. When I was in middle school, roughly equivalent to American high school, the Japanese leadership set as the nation's goal the establishment of a "Greater East Asia Co-Prosperity Sphere"—a large area of East Asia to be placed under Japanese hegemony. We thought this was a wonderful vision for our "superior" Japanese nation, and that we should dedicate ourselves, even at the cost of our lives, to attaining that goal.

A teenager imbued with such a vision naturally considers himself superior to the citizen of any other country. When he goes abroad, he does not expect to find any evidence of discrimination against himself, and does not make any special effort to look for it.

My initial reaction to America and Americans was that these "hairy foreigners" (an unfriendly Japanese colloquialism for Caucasians) had done rather well for themselves. Very soon my ignorance was replaced by a friendly interest, and then in time by affection.

Another reason I was not very conscious of discrimination, if any existed, was that I did my best to associate with Americans other than members of the Japanese community. The purpose of my coming to America, after all, was to learn about the country and its people. Ironically, because of the war, I found few other Japanese students with whom I might have spent time.

The third reason for my attitude was the philosophy I acquired after spending some time in the United States: Ultimately it is the individual who is important, not any particular category of human beings one is associated with. Because of this outlook, I was never annoyed by insults meant for the Japanese people as a group, which I viewed as totally irrelevant to me as an individual. I used to smile, saying to myself, "Me, 'treacherous'?" Yet I must admit that I did try to act in such a way as to give the lie to any such epithets. As far as I was concerned, war, which is an armed conflict between sovereign states, had nothing to do with personal relationships between individual citizens of warring nations.

Feeling that a record of my wartime life in America may be of interest to today's Americans, I have attempted to recount it as it happened, without making any moral judgments.

I did, however, change the names of some individuals to protect their privacy.

Prologue
June 1944

The Chicago field office of the FBI was famous for its anti-gangster drive in the 1930s that doomed such criminals as Al Capone, Machine Gun Kelly, and John Dillinger. In the early 1940s, however, it had a different mission: safeguarding the greatest military secret of the United States—or of all time.

Codenamed the Manhattan Project, the most vital part of the secret was located on the campus of the University of Chicago.

Under the leadership of Enrico Fermi, the Italian-born nuclear physicist, a team of hundreds of scientists worked in absolute secrecy to develop what would become the first nuclear weapon to be used in war. On December 2, 1942, the first manmade chain reaction of nuclear fission was achieved in a facility innocently disguised as a "Metallurgical Laboratory" under the stands of the university's athletic field.

By June 1944, most of the scientists involved had moved to Oak Ridge, Tennessee, to participate in the next phase of the Manhattan Project: the production of the bomb itself.

The Chicago field office's responsibility for protecting the super-weapon project had lessened. Still one day the staff received an unusual report it could not ignore.

The Provost Marshal's Office of Fifth Army Headquarters in Chicago had reported that a young Japanese man had persistently attempted to enroll at the university despite the fact that it was under U.S. Army orders not to admit Japanese students from the West Coast. The youth had arrived in the United States in late June 1941—only five months before Pearl Harbor—with a Japanese passport and a student visa issued by the U.S. Consulate General at Kobe.

When war came, he was living in San Francisco. The War Relocation Program carried out by the U.S. Army's Western Defense Command sent him to a relocation center in Arizona. But he was released after only nine months and reached Chicago in May 1943. His attempt to attend the University of Chicago from the September term that year was frustrated because of the Army ban. In January 1944, when the restriction was relaxed to permit American citizens of Japanese ancestry from the West Coast to enter the university, he had tried again. But he was still ineligible and was once again barred. The young man's unflagging persistence raised suspicions that this enemy alien was motivated by more than a desire for an education when he sought admission to the University of Chicago.

Although neither the FBI nor any other U.S. government agency had conclusive evidence, it had been rumored that the Japanese government had sent "thousands" of young Japanese men to the United States during the year before Pearl Harbor to carry out subversive activities once war started.

This Japanese "student" seemed to require thorough investigation. The Chicago field office director assigned Agent Orton to the case: Chicago File 100–15940.

The subject, Mr. Orton learned, lived at 1516 East Sixty-first Street—significantly, very near the university campus.

About 9:30 a.m., June 19, Agent Orton stood outside the residence not far from the Fifty-ninth Street station. The white, three-story wooden building in need of paint was adjacent to the tracks of the Illinois Central Railway. Morning glories were in bloom in a flowerbox on the edge of the porch, their vines clinging to cords fanning downward from the eaves.

Mr. Orton climbed two steps to the porch, walked across it and pushed the doorbell. A few moments later, a young Oriental man emerged from the shadowy hall.

"Is Mrs. Rasmussen home?" Mr. Orton inquired, mentioning the owner's name.

"No," the young man replied. "She is in California."

"Are you Murata, by any chance?" the agent asked, producing an I.D. card from his inside jacket pocket. "I am from the FBI."

"Yes, I am Murata."

Thus began the longest day—June 19, 1944—of my seven-year sojourn in the United States.

Dreaming of America

Fifty years ago, the average Japanese child had merely a vague notion that America was a big, rich country thousands of miles away. But I knew a little more about that distant land, because of my great-uncle Zenbei.

My sisters and I called him "American Grandpa," but he was actually our mother's uncle. Zenbei Murata had gone to California when he was in his early twenties, toward the end of the last century. He went through the usual hardships that confronted a Japanese immigrant on the West Coast of the United States in those years, but by 1930, Zenbei had established a successful nursery business in San Leandro, south of Oakland. Every few years, he would return to Japan to visit his mother and give us children American goodies such as chocolate kisses, Sunkist oranges, Spam, and Carnation condensed milk. Through the colorful Sunday newspapers with which the cartons were stuffed, I became familiar with such comic-strip characters as Mickey Mouse, Betty Boop, Donald Duck, Kaptain Katzenjammer's Kids, and Popeye.

Zenbei's last trip home took place in early 1934; he died of a heart ailment in April of that year. Before his death, Zenbei had told me that when I was older, if I wanted to study in America, his wife, Kané, would gladly be my guarantor. Only a sixth-grader at the time, I had no notion of the impact this suggestion might have on my life.

After finishing primary school in our home village, I went on to Ono Middle School, which was located two and a half miles away in the town of Ono. Although at this school for boys, as at all other middle schools, English was a required subject, it was in all respects totally alien to Japanese students. Mastering it seemed impossible. Three hours every week were devoted to this subject, but even after the five years of middle school, no student was expected to speak English or understand it when it was spoken by a native speaker. Throughout our years in the rural school, we students never saw an Englishman or an American unless we went to Kobe or other large cities. The only English we heard spoken by a native speaker was that of the British announcer on NHK's daily five-minute English-language news broadcast. Even our English teachers were unable to understand this news program.

Nevertheless, this formidable foreign language fascinated me, and I studied it with as much perseverance as I did all other subjects. To think that every person in America spoke this difficult language was mind-boggling. In school the students must study every subject in English. Fantastic, I thought.

During the first three years of my five-year middle school curriculum, however, I did not seriously contemplate placing myself in that language environment—America. Under the prewar educational system of Japan, the normal course followed by high achievers in middle school was to enter high school (the U.S. equivalent of the three-year high school in prewar Japan is the last year of senior high school and the first two years of the four-year college) and then go on to an imperial university. Having placed at the top of the class at the end of my third year at Ono Middle School, I had set my mind on this path.

But when my fourth year began, I developed pleurisy and was laid up for nearly the whole year. I returned to school after recovery to join the class behind me. Then, when I was preparing for an entrance exam for high school, I learned to my distress that no high school would accept an application from someone with a history of lung disease.

Now I had to change my plans. The only course open, however, was to aim at matriculation in a school lower in prestige than a high school. This was a demoralizing prospect. But one day it dawned on me that this setback offered a wider horizon: Freed of my preoccupation with a conventional goal, I could now aim to study in the United States.

While I was convalescing, a distant relative of ours had returned from America. He had told me it was not very difficult to work one's way through school in the United States because the cost of living was low while wages were high. He had done this himself to earn an engineering degree at the University of California. Studying in America no longer appeared a wild dream.

I recalled Uncle Zenbei's offer of financial support for my education. As a young boy, I had found the offer tantalizing merely because America appeared to be a glamorous and wealthy nation. But in middle school I learned to disdain such dreams of luxury. According to the prewar ethics of Japan, of which the ascetic elements of Confucianism were a key ingredient, true honor came from seeking out difficult situations and overcoming them. This provided me with an entirely different motivation for going abroad: As a student in a foreign country, I would be constantly challenged by hardships due to linguistic and cultural differences. Even the simplest of tasks would be a trial. If I could persevere through such an ordeal for four years or more, I would be more than prepared for any future adversity in my home country.

There was another attraction to this notion. My relative's stories had led me to believe that I could finance my own education. Doing so would mean one more rare achievement, and would be particularly meaningful because my parents would not be able to afford my tuition and living expenses abroad.

There was a Japanese word for this—working one's way through school—*kugaku*, literally meaning "learning by hardship." I had heard of people doing this because their parents were poor, and had always regarded them as heroes. In fact, the word itself had an aura of romanticism for me.

As I became more and more excited about this possibility, however, objective circumstances were turning steadily worse. Reading the newspaper delivered to our home, I got the impression that the relationship between Japan and the United States was fast deteriorating. I felt I needed someone to counsel me on the international situation with a clear perspective. But whom could I, a teenager in rural Japan, call upon?

Soon I found what I thought was the perfect answer. One Mr. Kinuji Kobayashi, a member of the Imperial Diet from our electoral district, was a family friend. He had studied in the United States and earned a law degree. Furthermore, he had once been private secretary to Yosuke Matsuoka, the influential politician who served as foreign minister in 1940 and later in 1941. The only problem was how to see him in Tokyo without absenting myself from school and financially burdening my parents.

A fortuitous development solved this problem, too. Because of my bout with pleurisy, I had been forbidden by my doctor to engage in kendo, a required martial arts course I started to take in the first year. So, when I returned to school, I joined the rifle club instead. Then, in October 1940, I placed fourth in a prefectural shooting match. Thus, as a member of our five-man prefectural team, I qualified to participate in the national athletic meet held annually in Tokyo on or around November 3 to celebrate the birthday of Emperor Meiji. This meant I could go to Tokyo on official business.

When I met Mr. Kobayashi, he heartily endorsed my plan of studying in America. He assured me there was no need to concern myself about the possibility of war between the United States and Japan because "we are working hard to avert it, and neither country gains anything from war." His reassurance was more than sufficient to make up for the disappointment I had felt about my poor score at the shooting range. It also greatly diminished my parents' reluctance to let me go.

After speaking to Mr. Kobayashi, I succeeded in persuading my parents to agree to my plan to study in the United States. I then set about obtaining a passport from the Japanese government and a visa from the American consulate in Kobe.

The requirements, essentially, were two documents. One was an affidavit from a guarantor who would pledge to pay for my educational expenses in America. I would ask my Aunt Kané for this, as Uncle Zenbei had suggested. (She lived comfortably in San Leandro on income from the nursery she had inherited from her late husband). The other was a letter from a school that was prepared to accept me. I described the requirements to Aunt Kané and asked her to locate a high school in her area that would provide the transition to college-level work. My plan was to study English at such a school and apply for admission to a university when I was ready. As I prepared to obtain these two documents, I felt I had to hedge against the possible international developments that might kill my plan. In early April 1941, I therefore enrolled at the Osaka University of Commerce after passing a competitive entrance examination. If I should fail to achieve my dream, I could stay on at this school.

On April 17, I received the affidavit from Aunt Kané as well as a letter from Mr. John Drew, principal of Drew School in San Francisco. According to the letter, Drew School was a private high school and a prep school for the University of California which also accepted foreign students who wanted to acquire English proficiency before entering an American college or university. I could now count on realizing my plan. On the following day, I went to see the dean of students of Osaka University of Commerce, Professor Yasuaki Okamoto, to tell him that I wanted to withdraw from the university.

"Withdraw?" the dean asked incredulously. "You attended the admission ceremony only a few days ago, didn't you? Why do you want to leave so soon?"

"I want to go to America to study. I now have prospects of getting a passport."

My remark seemed to further astonish and even anger the dean.

"To America?" He collected himself after a few seconds and then intoned: "Don't you know that our relations with the United States have now reached a flash point?"

This was news to me. Earlier in the month I had written to Mr. Kobayashi once again, seeking his views on the international situation. He sent me without delay a long scroll letter done with a writing brush. The gist of the missive was that he believed there would be no war. But this time, his letter contained a new element. "Nowadays," he wrote, "it is dangerous even to say there will be no war between Japan and the United States. Therefore, please burn this letter after you have read it."

I said with conviction to Dean Okamoto: "I don't believe there will be war."

The dean did not elaborate on his "flash point" statement.

"In any event, we won't allow you to leave school even if you want to."

Despite the dean's disapproval of my plan, I absented myself from classes to begin the process of obtaining a passport and visa.

And I did receive my passport—on May 11—from the prefectural government, which, under the centralized administrative system of prewar Japan, acted as a local agent for the central government.

Years later, many persons, including the FBI agents in Chicago, were curious about why the Japanese government issued me a passport as late as May 1941, when Japan was presumably already preparing for war against the United States. It now seems that as far as the Foreign Ministry was concerned, there was no reason not to issue me a passport.

Likewise, the United States Consulate in Kobe, it appeared, had no reason not to give me a visa when I met all the requirements. The visa I received noted that I was to be admitted to the United States as a "nonquota immigrant" and that I was the twenty-fourth person to receive such a visa in that year.

With all the procedures now completed, I immediately booked a second-class passage on the *Kamakura Maru*, scheduled to leave Kobe on June 11. The fare of ¥1,100, the equivalent of about $250 today, was paid for by my mother with savings she withdrew from her bank.

In 1941, Japan's rainy season began punctually, bringing torrents on the night of June 10. About eleven o'clock on the following morning, I climbed the rain-soaked gangplank of the 17,500-ton luxury liner of Nippon Yusen Kaisha (NYK), berthed at the Fourth Pier of Kobe Port. Raindrops splattered on the water between the quay and the ship's side. Beneath the oil slicks, I saw a single jellyfish hanging suspended just beneath the surface.

At last, I was on my way to America. I wore the dark blue uniform of the college division of the Osaka University of Commerce. My head was covered by a regulation black visor cap, circled with two white stripes. My uniform was made of a synthetic textile called "staple fiber," a precious artificial cloth developed in the resource-scarce Japan of those years. My shoes were new but made of horsehide, another substitute material that made up for the shortage of cowhide, caused by the expanded demand from the Army. Under my arm I carried an attaché case made not of leather but cardboard, containing my passport and other important papers. I was a living example of the state of resources in the Japan of mid-1941, which was fighting its "holy war" in an attempt to establish the Greater East Asia Co-Prosperity Sphere. The prolonged war in China was sapping the nation of its economic strength and precious manpower.

My mind flashed back to more than twenty-four hours before. On the morning of June 10 I had taken a seven-minute walk to the nearest station, Kawai Nishi, which was on the private train line called Bantan Railways. On its single track crossing the Harima Plain, diesel-powered trains consisting of two or three cars and longer freight trains pulled by a locomotive ran several times a day.

The passenger train I boarded started moving southward after a horn signal. Within a minute it was running near my home, which was only one hundred yards away. I could see my great-grandmother, eighty-seven years old, waiting for my train in front of our house by the long, roofed wall that shielded our landscape garden. In front of her stood my four-year-old baby brother, Kazushige. Like most elderly Japanese women of those years, she had a bent back. She did not have to stoop; her face was naturally close to Kazushige's.

I could almost hear her say, "That's your big brother's train," though I knew Kazushige did not quite comprehend the significance of the situation. He would not see me for an unknown number of years. Maybe five, six years or even longer, I thought. And I would not see him again as an adorable, full-of-fun four-year-old. As for my great-grandmother, the chances were, I thought, that this would be the last glimpse I would have of her.

At Sannomiya Station in Kobe I met by arrangement with Osamu Matsusue, one of my former classmates. Before graduation from middle school, he had taken the entrance examination of the military academy, Japan's West Point, and failed. He was planning to spend a year preparing for another try. We went to a nearby hotel where my father had rented a room for two nights. It so happened that he, a primary school principal, was to attend a two-day conference in the prefectural capital. As the three of us had dinner together, I wondered how many years would elapse before we would do this again. After dinner, Matsusue left us for his house, promising to meet us at the pier on the morrow.

Back at the hotel, I checked the contents of my briefcase, which included a white folding fan. It held eight *waka*, thirty-one-syllable poems, that my mother had composed and inscribed in traditional fluid script with excellent calligraphic skill. These poems lyrically expressed sentiments of a mother sending her son to a distant and strange country and wishing him good luck and success in attaining his goal despite great odds. As I read them over again silently, I was overcome with emotion. I put the fingers of my right hand over my forehead to shield my moist eyes from my father's view. But he asked, "What's that?" Evidently he knew nothing of the poems.

"Just a fan," I managed to say, trying hard not to betray my emotion.

When we awoke the following morning, it was still raining hard and very windy. We had breakfast together in the station restaurant. My father had to attend the second-day sessions of the conference, which would last until noon.

"I can't come to the pier to see you off," he said. "So, good luck."

In a Japanese parting, there are no hugs, handshakes, or touching. All thoughts and feelings are conveyed with a few words—often even without them. Apart from such a tradition, I was embarrassed to say anything special. I did not even wave my hand as my forty-seven-year-old father climbed the stairs to the train platform.

At the prefectural government building, he was seized with a desire to see his son again at the pier. He told the official in charge his special reason for wanting to be excused. Not many head-masters had their sons leaving for America in those months,   and my father was readily let out. He hailed a cab in front of the   government building.

"Fourth Pier," he told the driver, hoping to be able to make it before the ship set sail at noon.

It was nearly one o'clock when the *Kamakura Maru*, with her moorings slipped and anchors weighed, finally blew her whistle. The band of white-uniformed musicians stationed near the bow on the second-class deck struck up the "Battleship March," heralding the departure. Formerly the usual music for parting in Japan was "Auld Lang Syne," but it had been replaced by the martial melody during the war years. The words of the march sang of a mighty armada to defend the empire and to assail any country that might do it harm.

Another sign of the times was the conspicuous absence of the paper tape, a familiar prop at a ship's departure, serving as the last lingering link between those aboard the vessel and those on shore. Japan was so short of pulp that use of tape for such a purpose was considered a "luxury" to be eliminated.

As the music played, I looked out at the group of my relatives and friends assembled on the pier. My father had made it from the conference, just in time for a final farewell before I boarded the ship. My mother and elder sister had come from home in the morning of the same day. Including my kin and some friends and former teachers, my well-wishers numbered fifteen, a rather large group on that gray day.

Suddenly, I heard "Kiyoaki, *banzai!*" shouted by my maternal uncle, Isao Tamada. I could see tears well up in my mother's eyes.

As if not to be outdone, Matsusue shouted, "Hang in there, Murata!"

Without responding verbally, I produced from my jacket pocket a small Rising Sun flag and extended its aluminum pole to wave it. It was a gift from Aunt Yoshiko, my mother's younger sister from Osaka; I was her favorite nephew. She had given me another flag, a regular-sized one folded in a small paulownia-wood box. Their symbolic meaning was obvious: I was not to lose my Japanese soul while in a foreign country.

The *Kamakura Maru* was now gliding backward—first almost imperceptibly, but then the space between the ship and the quay widened. As she continued to move away, I edged toward the bow, trying to find a break in the row of passengers lining the railing, to show myself to my people—all the while waving the flag. The rain had stopped but there were strong winds. I feared that the aluminum pole of the flag might bend or snap against the gales.

Before long, the ship was so far from the quay that it was difficult to distinguish the faces of the people on the pier. But the red handkerchief my elder sister, Akiko, had sense enough to bring and wave was clearly visible. Aunt Yoshiko's wisteria-colored raincoat, too, stood out in the motley of dismal colors enveloped in the dampness of that gray June day.

Matsusue had run to the end of the pier as the ship steadily moved away and toward the breakwater. Though I was certain he no longer recognized me at this distance, he kept on swirling his raincoat as if to insist upon being there.

The ship finally came to a halt outside the breakwater. She was turned around by tugboats so that her bow would point east, and then under the ominously overcast sky, slowly at first, then gradually picking up speed, she began to plow the waters of the Inland Sea toward the Pacific Ocean.

Chapter

2

First Impressions

The *Kamakura Maru* docked at Yokohama at 5:00 p.m. on June 12. After unloading a large number of passengers from Shanghai and Kobe and receiving new ones bound for the United States, she set sail at 3:00 p.m. on June 14.

On my first seagoing journey, I was fascinated by the expanse of ocean surrounding the ship, white foam in its wake. Sometimes I would gaze out at albatrosses following the ship or a school of flying fish dancing on the waves in the distance.

The most remarkable feature of life on the ship was the food. I was dumbfounded by the large number of choices for each of the three meals and the fact that one could have any amount of any of them. To me, this was almost a sin. In Japan, food was becoming scarcer by the day, and the government was exhorting the nation about the need for economy and frugality with such slogans as "Luxury is our enemy," "luxury" meaning wanting to eat enough to fill one's stomach.

On the *Kamakura Maru*, there was not a hint of the situation at home. Everything seemed to reflect "luxury," including the fact that our bed linen was changed every other day. The sparkling white polished rice in a Japanese-style meal on the menu appeared unreal because in Japan few ate such rice. People were being encouraged by the government to eat either half polished rice or rice mixed with barley.

The second-class passengers numbered about thirty, the majority of them Americans who had left the Far East because of the deteriorating international situation. Even on my visits to Tokyo and Kobe, I had never seen such a large number of Westerners in one place. I was eager to speak to them, but despite my diligent studying, I found I was utterly unable to communicate in English. From time to time, I tried to make out what they were saying, but the American accent was so different from the British pronunciation I learned in school that it was incomprehensible. I realized that the years that lay ahead would be hard ones indeed.

There were several Japanese-Americans who had been living in Japan and a number of native Japanese who were permanent residents of the United States, returning to the West Coast after a visit to their home country. I engaged them in conversations in Japanese, asking them about America and Americans. When they learned that I was going to the United States as a student, they were first incredulous, and then amazed that the government of Japan had issued me a passport at all.

A ship's officer in NYK uniform trimmed with gold braid often joined us at the dinner table. When he learned of my plans, he remarked disdainfully, "There is nothing more to learn from America. Now Germany, of course, that's something else."

I chose not to dispute his opinion but told myself I was not going to America merely to gain knowledge, but more to make a man out of myself through the hardship of living abroad. Obviously, the officer did not have a very high opinion of Japanese students going to America—largely because of their motives. Most of those who entered the United States after completing secondary education in Japan did so because they had failed to enroll at a Japanese college. There were also many others who had used their student status to come to America after Congress restricted immigration from Japan in 1924.

I asked the officer about the son of a very well-known and influential noble family, who, I had read, had attended an Ivy League college. He had had to return home recently without being able to graduate because his conscription deferment was running out. It had been reported that he was a great golf enthusiast while in America.

"He spent every summer vacation back in Japan," the officer said. "He was on this ship, too. We used to laugh at him behind his back, saying, 'That stupid son of a nobleman is going home again.'"

This was amazing. I had left home with a pledge to myself never to return without accomplishing my objective. It had never occurred to me that even one Japanese student had gone home once every year. The travel time alone, back and forth across the Pacific and the continent, would have been at least a month and a half. I had planned to complete my study in the United States as quickly as possible so that I could come home to serve in the Army. As a male subject of the Emperor, I was required to fulfill three sacred obligations: military service, education, and payment of taxes. I had committed myself to the pursuit of my goal and I was not going to give it up come hell or high water. To return home without completing my self-imposed mission would be a disgrace worse than death, I felt. To visit home every summer seemed an act of apostasy.

As the ship neared Hawaii, the deck on which I spent most of my time with other young passengers became drenched by the sun's strong rays. One day I met a middleaged Japanese passenger who said he had come down to our deck from the first class deck because he didn't like the formality there.

Though he was in plain clothes, he was a military man—Captain Kyoho Hamanaka of the Imperial Japanese Navy on his way to Mexico City to serve as naval attaché at the Japanese Embassy there. He saw the uniform I wore and asked me which university I was attending. When I told him, he said, "Then you should have recognized me. I often give talks at the Osaka University of Commerce. I was stationed at the Naval Personnel Bureau in Osaka. If you don't know me, you must be a fake."

I said I had just entered the university in April and had been there for less than a month. The broad-shouldered naval officer accepted my explanation because he had not been at the university since before April.

But, he said jovially, "I didn't know there was a student from that university with enough guts to go to America to study at this time."

This I accepted as a compliment. I decided to forgive him for his jest that I might be a phony.

"Do you think there will be war between Japan and America?" I asked him, thinking that of all the people on the ship, he would be the most knowledgeable source on this subject.

"I don't think so," the naval officer replied with a smile. But somehow he did not sound entirely convincing.

Years later, I learned that Captain Hamanaka was on a vital mission to Mexico: to make a deal for the import of oil, the precious war materiel Japan desperately needed. But the captain failed because the Mexican government, under pressure from Washington, refused to sell oil to Japan.

On June 21, the day before we were due to arrive at Honolulu, the ship's mimeographed daily bulletin announced that Hitler's Germany had invaded the Soviet Union. The news cast a pall of gloom over the entire liner. Everyone was apprehensive about the future of Japan–United States relations. The steward in charge of our cabin darkly observed as he came to change linen, "There is no assurance that even this ship will arrive at San Francisco safely."

Another member of the crew said that if the *Kamakura Maru*, should hostilities break out in the Pacific, were seized by the United States government, "We would probably have to spend the war years farming in a detention camp somewhere in America."

The ship's officer at our table that night said that in case of war the NYK liner would be commandeered by the Japanese Navy to serve as a transport ship. He also said the two other NYK liners, Japan-built 19,000-tonners, were designed to be converted into aircraft carriers. When war did come, the *Kamakura Maru* was indeed turned into a transport ship and was later sunk. Years after the war, I was saddened to learn that the captain and crew lost with the ship had been the same as those I met on my trip across the Pacific. The two other liners, the *Nitta* and the *Yawata*, were converted and renamed *Chuyo* and *Unyo* respectively; they, too, were sent to the bottom of the ocean before the war was over.

Such talk aboard the ship, I had to admit, increased my concern. If hostilities should really develop after I arrived in the United States, what would become of me? What would it be like to live in a country with which my own was at war? With my meager worldly knowledge, I could find no answer. Instead, I saw myself walking toward a bank of fog that shrouded my immediate future as the *Kamakura Maru* ceaselessly plowed the waves eastward.

Eleven days after leaving Kobe, the ship arrived at Honolulu. One of my fellow passengers, a Hawaiian Nisei who had spent several years in Japan, offered to guide me around town. As we disembarked, we were surprised to see that the Japanese-Americans bound for the mainland were not allowed to leave the ship. The reason the immigration officers gave was that these Nisei had been in Japan for a long time and therefore would not be able to speak English well.

This did not seem to make sense because my command of English was hardly any better than theirs. Was the real reason simply a matter of discrimination between native-born Americans of Japanese ancestry and a student from Japan? I wondered if students were considered to have a higher social status than Nisei, and if disembarking at Honolulu was a privilege only accorded to certain classes of people.

Four decades after June 1941, it occurred to me that perhaps there was another, unspoken reason: The United States government, or at least the military authorities in Hawaii, might have felt that the returning Nisei had been assigned some intelligence missions to perform in Honolulu in preparation for the war Japan had planned.

Early in the morning of June 18, the *Kamakura Maru* entered San Francisco Bay. After dressing hastily, I rushed to the deck, expectant and elated. America! The NYK liner, moving incessantly eastward, had finally borne me across the great blue ocean over a distance of more than six thousand miles. Now, beyond a few more miles of water, stood a clutch of skyscrapers against the cloudless morning skies. Perhaps because of the early hour, nothing seemed to stir. The calmness gave the scenery an unrealistic appearance, like that of a film studio backdrop.

As I finished a breakfast of cornflakes and scrambled eggs at the end of the fourteen-day voyage, I was assailed by a bittersweet feeling. Even though I was eager to go ashore to America, I didn't exactly feel like leaving the ship. I had been spoiled by the life of "luxury" and comfort.

Disembarkation procedures began when immigration officers came aboard and set up a temporary office on the deck with tables and chairs. The officer who checked my papers found them in order and produced a mimeographed sheet. He noted on it the date of entry and the name of the ship and told me to read the instructions carefully. This information sheet quoted a section of the Immigration Act of 1924 concerning students, of whom there were three classes: (1) a student whose parents or relatives could finance his education; (2) a student who had insufficient income to cover necessary expenses; and (3) a student having no means whatsoever.

In the blank space following "Class" in the sentence immediately below the instructions, the immigration officer entered "1." I quickly looked up at the instructions and discovered that Class 1 students were forbidden to become gainfully employed. I would not be allowed to work to finance my own education! This seemed to undermine the very essence of my ambition to face the challenge of *kugaku*. What had I come all this way for, if I wasn't going to be permitted to face that challenge? But I could not protest, and in fact, as I realized later, without a guarantor I simply would not have been issued a visa in the first place.

After paying a customs duty of one dollar and seventy cents, I entered the United States of America a free man. I was met on the quay by my great-aunt Kané. She was accompanied by Mr. Shimizu, the nursery manager, and his wife. Mr. Shimizu had worked for Uncle Zenbei for years and had served as manager of the nursery since Zenbei's death in 1934.

I was taken to Chinatown for lunch. It was strange and even somehow discomfiting to be confronted by a section of the American city filled with Chinese signs and Asian faces hardly distinguishable from Japanese.

We started for San Leandro by crossing the Bay Bridge. As we passed through the toll booth at its Oakland end, Mr. Shimizu paid the twenty-five cents to the uniformed policeman who, I noticed, wore a revolver in his hip holster. I was astounded to hear him say "Thank you" upon receiving the toll. A policeman saying "Thank you" to a civilian for performing his official duty? From a Japanese point of view it was fantastic.

"Well, this is democracy," Mr. Shimizu explained with a chuckle when I indicated my astonishment.

We stopped at a department store in Oakland, which I found very tidy, clean, and quiet, and not as crowded as those in Kobe. Aunt Kané outfitted me with American clothes from head to toe: a hat, a dark blue suit with a spare pair of trousers, a dress shirt, and a pair of shoes made not of horsehide but cowhide.

From Oakland we headed south for the small town of San Leandro. Aunt Kané's house and rows of greenhouses stood in the midst of open space, surrounded by vegetable fields.

The white-painted two-story house I had seen pictures of back home looked modern and comfortable. The ground floor consisted of a dining room, a kitchen, and a large storage space. At a corner of it was a Japanese-style bath, Uncle Zenbei's own idea. The second floor comprised a living room with a player piano and several bedrooms. One with a single bed and a dresser had been prepared for me. The bathroom here, adjacent to the master bedroom Aunt Kané used, featured a shower.

I had heard about and expected the facilities and arrangement of the house. The most amazing feature of it, however, was running hot water. Even running cold water was a luxury in rural Japan, but running hot water! The standard of living I witnessed here in what seemed to be a very ordinary American-style house could be found only in the homes of the very wealthy in Japan.

I began attending Drew School on July 7, 1941, nine days after disembarking from the *Kamakura Maru*. The night before my first solo trip to San Francisco, I discussed with the Shimizus the question of what I should do if someone started speaking to me in English. Mrs. Shimizu, who was an American citizen, taught me the sentence I should use. I practiced it carefully, repeatedly, paying attention to each vowel and consonant in the brief sentence.

The next morning, with textbooks and a paper bag containing sandwiches, I boarded the orange-colored Key System bus at the nearest bus stop in town. In this, my first experience on an American bus, I was surprised by the joviality of the driver, who greeted each boarding passenger with a hearty "Good morning!" It appeared that life was simply wonderful and he had absolutely nothing to complain about. As days passed, I began to feel that the driver was not an exception: Most other Americans appeared just as happy and content.

There were many other striking things about American buses. They were roomy, clean, and comfortable. And there were always seats for passengers, no one having to stand up in the aisle.

On my first ride, almost as soon as I sat down, a male passenger, a thirtyish, light-complexioned man with a black moustache, began speaking to me. Whether he was trying to find an answer to a question or simply being sociable, I was unable to tell. In any event, I had an answer that could not fail.

I said: "I have just come from Japan, so I can't speak English."

My practice paid off because my neighbor stopped speaking. Yet he appeared puzzled—for good reason. He was told that I could not speak English. But I was actually contradicting myself, for he clearly understood the English sentence I spoke.

At Drew School, I was late for the first class, and Mr. Drew, the principal, personally escorted me to Room 11 on the second floor. As the door was opened, I saw a small class of about ten pupils about fifteen years old—boys and girls together! This was an amazing sight to me. Coeducational high school was absolutely inconceivable at that time in Japan, where the Confucian adage, "Boys and girls after seven must not be seated together," was strictly observed. The teacher, who was introduced to me as Mr. Judge, was tall, ruddy-faced, and handsome in a dark blue suit, and above all, very kind. He appeared to be in his late twenties. Receiving me from Mr. Drew, he led me, with his hand protectively on my back, to an empty seat in the back of the room.

The class was English I. The pupils were studying the basics of English grammar, at a level I had mastered several years earlier at school in Japan.

I found Mr. Judge the most articulate American—in terms of pronunciation—I had encountered so far and perhaps since. I was able to understand practically everything he said.

But not so with other teachers. In the mathematics class that followed English I, Mrs. Rambo, a middleaged woman who was conspicuously thin, explained algebra also at a level I had gone through years before. But I did not understand a single word she uttered in her continuous outpouring. After the class was dismissed, I stood out in the hall dejected, on the verge of tears.

"How can I ever hope to reach my goal at this rate?" I asked myself. All my high hopes for this great expedition of mine—working my way through school in America and coming home with a college degree in hand—now seemed to have been violently shattered. The situation was no better in the physics class, where the teacher was even less intelligible than Mrs. Rambo because he mumbled.

Mr. Judge's class was the only bright spot in my life at Drew School. It was largely because, surprisingly enough, I proved a "superior" student in one respect. I did better than anyone else in the class as far as grammar was concerned. It was almost amusing to find

American teenagers unable to tell what was wrong with sentences like, "It was him who called on you yesterday" and "This book is different than that book."

Within a few days of my having joined the class, Mr. Judge told me to sit in a row closer to the front—between two girls, Audrey, a blonde, and Ramona, a brunette. I had not quite become accustomed to the concept of coeducational school to begin with, much less myself sitting between two young girls. Yet I found the new location pleasant. The teacher's reason for placing me there, however, was, as he explained to the class, strictly pragmatic. He wanted me to serve as a barrier between the two girls, who talked to each other too often. For that purpose, Mr. Judge could not have found a better pupil.

One day, the teacher asked me where I had lunch. I said I ate sandwiches on the bench in the schoolyard.

"I will have my mother make me sandwiches starting tomorrow. Then we can talk to each other, and you can practice speaking."

After lunch in the schoolyard, Mr. Judge would walk with me in the neighborhood—one day to take me to a corner drugstore where I learned how to buy a Coke or a magazine and on another to a public library, where he explained to me the system of people obtaining library cards. He had me registered with the librarian, serving as my reference, so that I could check books out.

During one of these walks, Mr. Judge produced an apple from his pocket and began munching away at it. I was dumbfounded. In Japan, eating while walking was considered extremely rude. It was jarring to see a gentleman like Mr. Judge engaging in such shocking behavior. During those weeks, the more I saw of American culture, the more unfathomable it became.

The Darkening Skies

My first experiences with English comprehension on the *Kamakura Maru* had been a good indication of what was to come. Despite my command of English grammar, my capability in dealing with spoken English was practically nil. In San Francisco, I knew the language people were speaking was English, but it hardly sounded like it to my ears.

A few days after I settled down in Aunt Kané's house, Mr. Shimizu took me to a movie being shown in town at a theater called the Rialto.

The film was *Caught in the Draft*, featuring Bob Hope. The comedy was about a young man, played by Hope, who is drafted into the Army. Because of the crises he creates wherever he goes, he is transferred from one branch of the service to another.

The story and its comic nature were obvious. Nonetheless, it was discouraging that the only part of the dialogue I understood, aside from occasional monosyllabic words like "yes," "no," or "hey!" was a single sentence spoken slowly for emphasis by an irate colonel to Private Hope, who tries unsuccessfully to explain how he happened to be in WAC quarters: "I—don't—understand—what—you—say!"

While I thoroughly enjoyed the comic part of the film, I was astounded by one element of it: When the hero is ordered to report to the draft board under the Selective Service System Act of 1940, he does his best to avoid being drafted. He even leaps from the top of a dresser to deliberately, though unsuccessfully, sprain his ankle.

Conscription in Japan was a sacred duty of all male Japanese, and any attempt at evading it was treasonous and met with severe penalties. Yet in America, I found, a whole movie could be made about such a crime. In this sense, *Caught in the Draft* provided me with a precious lesson in democracy.

A few days later, I was taken to another movie, *That Hamilton Woman*, starring Laurence Olivier as Lord Nelson and Vivian Leigh as his mistress. Here the dialogue was much more intelligible to me because it was British. I saw that the famous quote "England expects that every man will do his duty" was a message Nelson sent to his fleet by a flag code signal, and I was able to anticipate the line he spoke on his deathbed, which I had learned in Japan: "Thank God, I have done my duty."

Letters from my parents and friends assuaged my homesickness and pains of struggle with the English language. One or two more ships from Japan had docked at San Francisco since the *Kamakura Maru*, and each time, a day or so later, letters from Japan were delivered to me.

On July 23, 1941, President Franklin Roosevelt announced the freezing of Japanese property in the United States as a means of retaliation against the Japanese Army's plan to move into French Indochina (today's Vietnam).

Another NYK ship, the *Tatsuta Maru*, was due to dock at San Francisco on the following day, the twenty-fourth. I had been eagerly looking forward to the ship's arrival because I knew it would mean another bonanza of letters from home. But the liner failed to show up; in fact, it went "missing." Besides the *Tatsuta*, approximately fifty Japanese ships known to have been in the waters off the West Coast, including freighters and tankers, lost contact with shore.

The situation caused a small panic. Those who were expecting their kin and friends to return aboard the *Tatsuta* worried about the ship's fate. Yet the NYK liner remained silent and invisible.

NYK and the Japanese government presumably feared that the expensive passenger ship might be seized by the United States government once it arrived at San Francisco. That, however, was not my immediate concern. Nor did I know anyone aboard the missing liner. But the mail pouch—and the letters I knew were in it—was my only link to home and my family.

Every day on my way home I looked for the Tatsuta from the bus as it crossed the Bay Bridge. Every day I was disappointed. Then Washington announced it would not seize the ship. The newspapers said the government was announcing by radio—on a frequency the liner would pick up—that there was no danger of the ship being confiscated. "Come in, *Tatsuta*. We won't seize you," the message said in effect.

On July 30, Wednesday, as I left school, I went to a street-corner newsstand as usual to read the headlines of the afternoon papers. There it was: a picture of the *Tatsuta* in the bay. At the downtown terminal, I took a seat on the leftside row of the bus to make certain I could see the piers. Through a light haze, indeed I sighted the Japanese ship. As the bus sped on and my vantage point changed, I was now able to see the Rising Sun flag at its stern. After days of hiding in the fog bank off the coast, the ship had finally emerged. To me she was a living thing that had come from Japan, braving all hazards. Overwhelmed by sentiment, I put my face on my knees. Tears wet the cover of my textbook.

However, as if to dispel the relief we felt about the *Tatsuta*, another blow came on August 1. The United States government banned the export of oil and scrap iron to Japan. After this, the several Japanese freighters and tankers I used to see from the bus window rusting in San Francisco Bay vanished. They had come to load oil and scrap iron, the two precious war resources for Japan, and they went home with empty holds.

The *Tatsuta* came and went. The next NYK liner to cross the Pacific, the *Asama Maru*, left Yokohama on July 18 and entered

Honolulu on the thirty-first, five days later than scheduled. This was because of instructions by the Japanese Navy, which was evidently weighing the development of diplomatic discussions in Washington. The *Asama* left Honolulu on August 1 for San Francisco, but three days later, she turned back at midpoint—again as instructed by the Japanese Navy—and returned to Yokohama on August 10.

The traffic over the Pacific by Japanese ships thus came to a halt a little over a month after my arrival. I recalled the remark made by Dean Okamoto of the Osaka University of Commerce that the situation between the two countries was at a flash point. I had to admit that perhaps he had not been far off.

I had just made it—like running into a train a second before the doors closed. My conviction that there would be no war now began to waver. And I was beginning to have doubts about the wisdom of my decision to come to the United States. Still, I tried to reassure myself that efforts were being made in Washington for an amicable settlement of the issues.

On August 2, I received two letters that had evidently been brought by the *Tatsuta Maru* at the end of July. One of them was from Tadashi Fujiwara, my closest former classmate, who had enrolled at Tung Wen College in Shanghai, a Japanese college with emphasis on Chinese studies. The other was from another friend, Kinsuke Nishimura, who was at the Kobe pier when I left. He enclosed an English translation of *Senjinkun* (Code for Fighting Men) which had been issued in January 1941 by the then war minister, General Hideki Tojo. It was understood that the code was authored and issued by the Japanese Army leadership in view of the palpable signs of depravities among the members of the fighting forces of Japan noted in the recent years in China. The depravities were of two categories: (1) misbehavior toward civilians and prisoners of war and (2) the rising number of Japanese soldiers being taken prisoner themselves. The issuance of this new code of conduct was a tacit admission by the Japanese Army of the atrocities committed by its men against Chinese civilians and prisoners of war. Japanese soldiers being taken prisoner was a sign of low morale, because all Japanese fighting men had been taught that surrender was not acceptable. Any known POW in enemy hands was classified as "killed in action."

Nishimura's enclosure was the English translation of just the preface of this Army catechism, which my friend must have found somewhere, probably in a magazine for Japanese students studying English. He thought it might interest me for the simple reason that it was in English and I was studying this formidable foreign language in America. I glanced through the piece of writing without paying serious attention to it because the substance of the document was obviously not relevant to me. Naturally, I knew nothing specifically of the events in China that had resulted in its publication.

I appreciated the trouble my friend went to in copying out this code in his meticulous, almost feminine handwriting, and I saved it. I had no idea, however, that years later, some people in Chicago might take special interest in this copy of the *Senjinkun* in my possession.

Struggle with English

D rew School had a year-round program and my schedule was changed in mid-August. Mr. Judge's English I was replaced by English II. Instead of Mrs. Dinsdale's Special English, I was to take American History. The very thick textbook I received for this class gave me a sense of foreboding.

Mr. Judge's class was held in the same room, though at a different time. The students were a year or so older than in English I, and Audrey and Ramona were also promoted to the same class with me. In American History, given by a Mr. Spitzer, I was surprised to find a world map on the wall that had been prepared by the Japanese Ministry of the Navy. Later I was to learn that Mr. Spitzer had been in China; presumably he had picked up the map there.

On the following day, Mr. Judge told me that he had one session unoccupied from 10:20 A.M. and that he would spend those forty minutes with me in conversation practice. These sessions, in which Mr. Judge would ask me questions about myself and Japan, proved extremely effective.

At the same time, my answers to the questions were apparently almost fantastic to my teacher. On the first day our conversation went as follows:

"How big is the population of Japan?"
"About one hundred million."

"Whew! And how big is Japan itself?"

"It's about the size of California."

"Gosh, people must be living on top of one another. What made you come to America, Kiyoaki?"

"I came here to experience hardship by being away from home and my parents."

"Why do you want to have hardship? Isn't it better to have an easy life?"

"Unless one experiences hardship, one cannot become a strong man."

"You are what we call a stoic. Do you know the word—stoic?"

"Yes, I do."

"Do you want to go back to Japan when you finish your studies here?"

"Of course, and then enter the Army."

"Army? Do you like war?"

"No, I don't. But I want to be at the front."

"Why?"

"Isn't it good to have many kinds of difficult experiences?"

"I'm sorry, I can't agree with you," said my teacher, shaking his head with a suppressed smile on his ruddy face.

Another subject that amazed Mr. Judge was the code of conduct I had adhered to in Japan and the regulations that restricted our activities at Ono Middle School.

While walking with him on the sidewalk, for instance, I would tend to lag a few steps behind—not abreast of—him. Asked about this habit, I explained, "In the Orient, there is a rule that a pupil must walk three steps behind his teacher and never tread even upon his shadow. It would be disrespectful."

I told Mr. Judge that because of my rigid adherence to such a code, I was nicknamed *kunshi*, the Confucian model of the perfect moral man.

To my question of how this term might be translated into English, Mr. Judge expanded my vocabulary by offering an answer after a few moments of cogitation.

"I think a 'paragon of virtue' might be it."

Such dialogues going on every day seemed to have deeply interested Mr. Judge in the strange country called Japan, which had bred the freakish human being who was now his respectful pupil.

As of October 8, I began taking Mr. Judge's English III in place of algebra, besides English II. The new class was at a considerably higher level than English II. The textbook contained short stories by O. Henry, among other writers. At the Osaka University of Commerce we had read some of his stories, but there one story took two weeks to digest while at Drew School the pace was more like "The Gift of the Magi" for today, "The Last Leaf" for tomorrow, and so on. On each of the seven or eight pages that constituted a short story, I found about a dozen new words.

But O. Henry was a pushover compared with Irving S. Cobb, a rural humorist whose wit I was hardly equipped to appreciate. In his works, there were about two unfamiliar words in every line.

My schedule, furthermore, did not consist solely of Mr. Judge's English classes. American History was ten times tougher to grapple with.

Before going to the United States, I knew little about the subject. My knowledge of the country had essentially remained at the Sunday comics level. In school, nothing was taught about America—no geography, no history, not to mention political institutions. Democracy, for instance, infrequently heard or referred to, was almost a bad word in the Japan of those years—like the word "socialism." Average students knew the names of two American Presidents—Washington and Lincoln—and possibly the incumbent, Roosevelt. They would also have known that there had been a civil war several decades earlier, identified in Japanese as the "South-North War."

In this class, I found the reading assignments formidable. Every day I had to read twenty to thirty pages, on each of which I would encounter about thirty new words. I had to look them up in the dictionary I brought from Japan, which I always carried in my jacket pocket and kept on my desk in class. My constant use of this particular lexicon apparently irritated Mr. Spitzer. One day he came to my desk and said, "Do you know the best way for you to study English?"

When I could find no suitable answer, which he apparently had expected anyway, he picked up my pocket dictionary, raised it shoulder high and pronounced, "It is to throw this dictionary into San Francisco Bay. You can't study English with a dictionary. You do it with your mouth and ears. Translation doesn't help you."

I most certainly disagreed with the teacher and in fact I was mortified: I had not come to America to forget my Japanese while I was learning English. I wanted to acquire a bilingual capability before returning to Japan. I had to know what each new English word meant in my mother tongue. But of course I could not offer such an account of my motivation to Mr. Spitzer in English. So I remained silent.

Nonetheless, I was impressed with the fact that none of the students in the class laughed or said anything. This was another occasion that made me keenly aware of what I regarded as a laudable American trait—not laughing at or abusing someone for his failure.

After the irascible Mr. Spitzer demonstrated such disapproval of my dictionary, I discussed the matter with Mr. Judge. I was heartened to find him supporting me rather than his colleague.

In mid-September I had a talk with Mr. Drew about my status. The principal said that I should stay at the school for another year because my present English proficiency was hardly high enough for me to be admitted to a college. This I could not dispute, and yet I felt I could not afford to dawdle at Drew School too long, because I was in a hurry to go through with my plans and return home to be able to fulfill my patriotic duty of serving in the Army.

There were a number of Chinese boys at Drew School who were, like me, studying English. We became friends partly because of our common language handicap and also because I helped them with mathematics, when they had trouble solving what appeared to me to be ridiculously simple problems.

In speaking to them, I often used Chinese ideographs to supplement my use of English. During the study period one day in early October, I sat next to Henry, one of the Chinese boys, and discussed Japan's war in China in a whisper. Our discussion caught the attention of Mr. McGary, the exceedingly affable and polite homeroom supervisor, whose facial expression indicated his disapproval of our conversation.

We stopped talking but resumed our conversation during lunch hour. I told Henry that Japan was "fighting Chiang Kai-shek for the sake of the Chinese people"—the line the people of Japan were fed by the government and which I believed to be the truth. I was surprised to find that Henry stubbornly disagreed with me. In fact, he countered my argument by asking, "If the Japanese Army is fighting for the people of China, why do they do terrible things?" Henry, having come from Canton, said he had witnessed atrocities committed by Japanese soldiers there.

"Is this true?" I wondered. In Japan, I had never heard such reports. All soldiers had been portrayed as "brave" and "well-disciplined" fighting men.

Unable to express myself in English adequately, I wrote in Chinese characters: "The Chiang regime has been alienated from the Chinese people." Henry apparently understood what I meant to say and squarely contradicted me. When he intoned in English, "Our country will not be lost," I observed his usually pale cheeks become flushed. I respected his sentiment as I asked myself, "If foreign troops came into my country and ran amok, how would I feel?"

Such contacts with Chinese youths of my age constituted an education for me, because they opened my eyes to the reality of Japan's foreign policy regarding the rest of Asia.

During my middle school days, the government of Japan had

intensified its nationalistic education program, trying to instill in the minds of youngsters the notion of the Greater East Asia Co-Prosperity Sphere. We had been told over and over that East Asia must rid itself of Western influences in favor of Japan's leadership, under which all the East Asian peoples—Chinese, Mongolians, Koreans, and Manchurians—were to "live and prosper together."

One day during the first weeks of my life at Drew School, I had a puzzling experience. A small boy with curly black hair saw me in the hall on the second floor. He raised his right arm forward and said, "Heil Hitler!"

I knew what "Heil Hitler!" meant, but why these words should be directed toward me was totally incomprehensible.

I spoke to Mr. Judge, who explained that the boy was a French refugee from Occupied France named André. He hated Germany and consequently Japan, an Axis ally, and he must have learned where I came from.

"But don't pay any attention to him," Mr. Judge advised.

Back home, Hitler was considered a great leader after the conclusion of the Axis Alliance by Japan, Germany, and Italy. In such a Japan, people were kept totally ignorant of the genocidal policy of Nazi Germany. Now, in the United States, I was beginning to learn about Hitler. I also started to understand the reasons for the anti-Hitler graffiti carved all over the classroom desks and chairs at Drew School.

In late September, I received a letter from Dr. Chitoshi Yanaga, a Nisei faculty member of the University of California whom my relative who had studied there had suggested I contact. I had written to Dr. Yanaga soon after my arrival in California, enclosing a letter of introduction. Dr. Yanaga's response invited me to meet him for advice on my educational plans. He wrote that I should come to see him at his home in Berkeley on the night of Friday, October 1.

I took a streetcar from Oakland and got off at Ashby Avenue. I was terribly impressed by the fact that Dr. Yanaga, an American-born scholar of Japanese parentage, spoke perfect Japanese. And his advice turned out to be invaluable. He said I must not consider entering a college or university on the West Coast but, rather, I should enroll at a small college—preferably in the Midwest—where I would be the only Japanese student or at least one of a very few on the campus.

Large universities like his own or Stanford had hundreds of Japanese students, Dr. Yanaga explained. If I were to enroll at one of these schools, I would end up mingling with the Japanese students and consequently not learn English. At such universities, in fact, the Japanese students had formed their own clubs. Joining them would be a waste of my time, retarding my acquisition of English. If I did not join them, I would experience unpleasantness, he said. Either way, I would lose out.

He then gave me a list of five small Midwestern colleges, including William Jewell and Antioch, suggesting that I write to them, inquiring about admission.

Dr. Yanaga told me he was now teaching Japanese to young Naval officers at the university. He showed me samples of homework submitted by his pupils, written in Japanese. These amazed me because, like most other Japanese, I had believed that it was utterly impossible for foreigners to learn Japanese. Dr. Yanaga said that the Japanese language program, formerly conducted in Tokyo, was now being held at Berkeley because it had become difficult to continue in Japan.

Two days later, I sent off letters to three Midwest colleges, expressing my interest in matriculation. I felt I had moved one step closer to my ultimate goal.

Chapter
5

St. Francis Wood

When I was admitted to the United States in late June 1941 at the age of eighteen, I was classified as a Class 1 student, which meant I was not authorized to become gainfully employed. Later, however, I learned that there was no problem in my earning room and board so long as I went to a day school on a full-time basis. The Immigration and Naturalization Service, I was told, was tolerant of foreign students working as domestic help because they did not deprive American citizens of jobs.

Encouraged, I attempted to find such a job by contacting the Japanese YMCA in town. In mid-October, soon after I had sent the inquiry letters to the colleges, I was informed about a potential employer. I immediately went to the YMCA and accompanied an officer who handled such matters to St. Francis Wood, an exclusive residential area.

The prospective employer turned out to be Mr. Frank Temple, who worked at a bank. Mrs. Temple interviewed me at their spacious, well-appointed home, a few minutes' walk from the streetcar stop just outside the Twin Peaks tunnel. They had a son, Frank Junior, the same age as I—eighteen—who stayed during the week at an out-of-town college dormitory and returned home on weekends.

When Mrs. Temple said that one of the chores I was expected to perform was laundry, I asked, "Do you have a washing machine?"

"No, we don't, because we don't have very much laundry. We are a small family."

This surprised me. I had seen a washing machine, one of the American marvels unknown to most Japanese, at Aunt Kané's house, and assumed an affluent family like the Temples was sure to own one.

I spoke briefly with the YMCA man in Japanese and decided to accept this offer. Back in San Leandro that evening, I described the position to Aunt Kané and the Shimizus. Both Aunt Kané and Mr. Shimizu were happy that I would have the opportunity to learn English while living among Americans, and would have the experience of working at a Caucasian home. I was convinced that nothing could possibly go wrong.

The next day I returned with my suitcase, escorted by Mr. Shimizu in his car. Mrs. Temple gave me a list of chores: (1) get up at 7:00 A.M.; (2) put the percolator on a burner; (3) prepare a breakfast of buttered toast and scrambled eggs for Mr. Temple; (4) bring in the milk bottle and newspaper from the porch, putting the milk in the refrigerator and placing the newspaper on the dining room table; (5) serve Mr. Temple breakfast when he comes downstairs at 7:30 A.M.; (6) after Mr. Temple leaves for work, eat breakfast and clean up; (7) give breakfast to Blackie, the black dog in the basement; (8) after returning from school, clean up all the rooms, and help Mrs. Temple prepare dinner; (9) clean up after dinner.

I asked Mrs. Temple about her own breakfast and was amazed to be told she would sleep until about eleven in the morning and prepare it for herself.

The next day was my first day of employment. I performed the prescribed work in the morning and went to school. After returning home, I dusted the furniture in the living room. Toward evening, Mrs. Temple said she had purchased a carton of rice especially for me, knowing that I, a Japanese, would like it. Though I was not experienced in cooking rice, I made a rough guess at the right amount of water to match the quantity of rice I placed in a pot. It turned out to be palatable, so I placed it on the dining room table in the room beyond the pantry. In a few minutes Mrs. Temple brought the pot back to the kitchen, saying, "This is for you. We don't eat rice."

I was puzzled for a few seconds before something I had not thought of dawned on me: I was to eat alone in the kitchen because I was, after all, a servant. All along, I was naive enough to presume that I would be eating with the family. This notion was based on my experience with a maid we had at home, who ate with us. But, of course, ours was a rare exception. In most Japanese homes that could afford domestic help, servants ate separately from the family. In our case, the maid even shared a room with my great-grandmother like a member of our family.

In other respects, too, my life seemed full of pitfalls—and frustrations—because of my inexperience, ignorance, and not least of all, linguistic inadequacy. One thing, however, was clear: Any fears about my working for Caucasians would have been utterly groundless. I was above all a servant to them; my nationality made no difference whatever.

On my second day of work, I was ready to have my own breakfast after Mr. Temple left for work. Presently, I found the kitchen full of smoke, which I discovered issued from the blackened piece of bread in the toaster I had forgotten to turn off.

That afternoon I didn't get home until about four because I ran an errand of my own after school. Mrs. Temple appeared to have been waiting for me. The moment I returned home, I was told to iron a mountain of laundry. Then the other routines followed. When I staggered up to my own room after cleaning up the dishes and utensils, it was close to nine o'clock and I was dead tired. I was hardly in shape to do homework.

The job I had acquired supplied room and board and paid the carfare of one dollar and twenty cents per week, the first cash income I had earned in my life. Indeed, this was the kind of life I had longed for—hardships to accompany my study in America, just like the ones I had described proudly to my friends in Japan and to anyone else who seemed to envy me for being able to go to what they considered the land of luxury and easy living.

As a matter of fact, during the summer months I had fretted because I could not land such a job while I commuted to school from the comfort of Aunt Kané's home. Now that my dream had come true, however, I was not entirely certain I was man enough to take it.

On my third day of domestic service, after school, as I walked toward the front of the Temples' residence, I heard a car screech to a stop behind me and several people scramble out.

"Kiyoaki, do you live here?" a young, cheerful voice said.

I turned around and was surprised to find Andy, whom I knew from Mr. Judge's English class. The other four boys looked familiar too, though they were not in any of the classes I attended.

"No, I don't live here. I only work here," I said, slightly surprised by my own fluency. As Andy explained, these boys lived in this area and went to school in the maroon-colored coupe driven by one of them. They seemed to be genuinely pleased to find another Drew School student in their neighborhood.

When I was washing dishes after dinner that evening, the doorbell rang. I opened the door to find Andy and his group.

"We're going to a show downtown. Do you wanna come along with us?"

"I am still working. I cannot finish until about eight. Besides, I must ask if I can go."

Mrs. Temple said, "After your work is done, it's your own time."

Hearing her, Andy said, "Okay. We'll come back at eight."

They were back at eight sharp and I was ready. I sat in the back seat with three of them. They were all eager to be sociable. When Dick, the driver, kept turning back toward me to speak, Andy told him with a touch of authority, "You just drive. I'll do the talking with Kiyoaki." He explained to me, "Dick bumped into a streetcar the other day."

Dick did not miss the opportunity to address me.

"I just had a wrestling match with a streetcar."

"And who won?"

"The streetcar . . . because it's so big. I got a bump on my fore-head."

The boys wanted to have my agreement to the movie they had planned to see. It was to be *Sergeant York*, about which I knew nothing. Andy explained what the film was about, but I did not understand all the explanation. His "Bang! Bang!" at the end of a sentence, accompanying a gesture of aiming a gun, made me think it was probably a Western. Then I gathered it was not. Someone said it was about World War I. I knew about that war from history classes, but I had not known until then that the United States was involved in it.

"Were many American soldiers killed in the First World War?"

"Oh, quite a few."

The answer stumped me. "Quite a few" seemed to me to mean "very few." But somehow this did not fit the context, and it remained a puzzle for several months.

At the large theater on Market Street where the Gary Cooper movie was being shown, each of us obtained a ticket and went up to the balcony. Then a minor problem developed about who would sit on either side of me. Eventually it was decided that Andy should be on my right and George on my left. Andy gave me a piece of chewing gum and said, "Don't swallow; just chew it."

The story of the film was relatively simple to follow even though I was unable to understand much of the dialogue. It turned out to be a memorable night that was an object lesson in American friendliness.

My fourth day at work was a Saturday and I was to be kept busy all day according to our agreement. Besides the weekday routine, I had to clean up the bathroom and basement floor, Blackie's habitat. In the morning I had a minor fiasco. I put the percolator on a burner before trotting to the front door to pick up the milk bottle and newspaper. I reached for these two items at the end of the porch while holding the door ajar with my left foot. I had to stretch and when I finally managed to pick up the two items, my foot slipped from the half-open door, which then closed and locked itself.

I placed my hand into my trouser pocket where I carried the key during the week. On this particular day, however, I had failed to transfer the key to my work pants. Concerned about the percolator in which the water would soon be boiling, I tried to enter through a window. I circled the house, but all the windows were tightly locked. I peeped through the kitchen window and, sure enough, the percolator water was now boiling, emitting white steam. I had been told by Mr. Temple that when the hot water rose to the upper flask, the burner must be turned off. Otherwise, I remembered him telling me, the percolator would "explode." I even recalled the satisfaction I felt when I understood this particular verb. I decided to abandon the notion of gaining an unconventional entry into the house and pushed the doorbell. In a minute or two, Mr. Temple came downstairs in his nightshirt. He appeared surprised to find me, but returned upstairs after hearing my explanation, without complaining about my having awakened him. I rushed into the kitchen, managing to save the percolator in the nick of time.

October 20, Monday, was my first laundry day. I was to dispose of the week's wash for the entire family, which included the soiled clothes Frank Junior brought home from his dormitory. And all this had to be done manually, as Mrs. Temple had told me during the interview. Doing washing for other people was another first for me. One thing I found almost intolerable was the fact that Mr. Temple apparently observed the policy of not using tissue paper for blowing his nose. There were about twenty handkerchiefs that had served the function of Kleenex.

About ten days after I began working for this family a real fiasco was to bring my career to a premature end.

On October 25, Saturday, the Temples were invited out to dinner, and I was told to prepare just my own supper. When I saw Mrs. Temple dressed up in her gorgeous evening gown, "It's beautiful," came to my lips quite naturally, testifying to my slowly developing linguistic capability. Pleased with this ingenuous compliment, Mrs.

Temple beamed and said, "Thank you." They went out a happy couple.

So far, so good. Now that I was all by myself in the large house I was seized with a strange sense of excitement, like that a speleologist might feel before entering a newly discovered cave. I had developed an insatiable curiosity about a button on the wall near the door of the master bedroom, which either of the two occupants would push from time to time. Each time, the small green light that usually glowed was replaced by a red light. But after a while it would give way to the green again. Unfortunately, I had not had this phenomenon explained.

Now I had the opportunity to unravel the secret myself: Just what happened when the button was pushed and what lay behind the mystery?

I pushed the button and saw the green light go out and the red one go on. But I observed no other change. Nothing seemed to happen. Perhaps, I thought, I did not push the button hard enough. I gave it another push—harder this time. Still nothing. I was disappointed. I had expected something spectacular, like music starting or a mouse leaping out.

I went up to my room to study. After a while, I felt all was not in order. Coming down to the master bedroom, I found it excessively warm, and the light remained red. Then I knew the answer: The button had turned on the heater. The little red lamp indicated that the burner was on somewhere in the house, funneling hot air into the bedroom. Not knowing what I should do except to open the windows, I again went back to my room to study.

At about eleven o'clock, Frank Junior returned home from school. The moment he came in, he said, "Kiyo, don't you smell something burning?"

"I can't smell very well because my nose is not good," I said.

Frank ran down to the basement. After a few minutes, he came up to my room and said the boiler in the basement, having been on for four to five hours, was red hot.

The following morning I apologized to Frank Junior and offered to pay for the burnt-out transformer. But Frank said there was no need for that. "Take a lesson from this experience." Mr. and Mrs. Temple said nothing to me.

The following Saturday, November 1, Mr. Temple phoned from the office to say that he had invited two important guests for dinner. After returning home, he himself helped prepare for the dinner to be served in the formal dining room, which was not usually used. To take down the expensive tableware from a high shelf, he needed a stepladder. He told me to bring it but I did not understand him. For the first time I saw him lose his temper. He shouted, "Ladder!" Then he still had to get it himself because I did not know where the ladder was stored.

At breakfast on November 5, Mr. Temple told me I was being fired—though not in so many words. But I was able to understand what he was driving at when he said he had found someone who understood English better than I and who could work on a full-time basis.

I was elated by this dismissal notice. At the same time, I could not help sympathizing with the Temples for having put up with me for as long as they did while I managed to make a series of errors, including the major one that almost burned the house down. Furthermore, I knew I must have appeared dour and haughty. I simply did not fit the role of servant.

On the following day, I was picked up by Mr. Shimizu and left St. Francis Wood. I knew I would miss the charming environment in which I had lived for eighteen days—of homes with white walls and red roofs, surrounded by green lawns and trees. And I would never forget the evenings when the famous San Francisco fog would creep up from the sea, casting a dreamlike veil on the landscape.

On November 7, Friday, I boarded the same Key System bus that I had ridden until three weeks before from San Leandro to San Francisco. The same genial driver and the same passengers were there, including the man with the black moustache who had attempted unsuccessfully to strike up a conversation with me on my first ride in early July.

Chapter
6

The Surprise Attack

Within a week after having lost my job in St. Francis Wood, I was able to land another only a few blocks from school. My new employer was a Mr. Hammond, a refined gentleman who lived with his wife and a son about two years old. My duties at the Hammonds' essentially involved helping Frieda, a hardworking young maid of German descent from Montana. On weekends I did housecleaning under her supervision.

On Wednesday, November 19, at the end of the class, Mr. Judge asked his pupils with a straight face, "By the way, today is the birthday of a very famous person. Do you know who?"

The pupils mentioned Washington, Rockefeller, Longfellow, Whitman, and so on. But the teacher kept saying no, while appearing to have increasing difficulty suppressing a smile.

"He is a very famous international diplomat," he said, to give a subtle clue. In my naiveté, I did not have the vaguest idea whom he had in mind.

"Lloyd George?" was one last try. Then all gave up.

"Kiyoaki!" Mr. Judge said.

Merry laughter filled the room, everyone saying "Happy Birthday!" to me. They asked me how old I was. When I said nineteen, they were surprised because they thought I was about fifteen —their own age.

On that day, when I awoke in my increasingly chilly basement room at the Hammonds' residence, I knew that at home my mother would be cooking rice with red beans, as is customary on happy occasions like birthdays. I knew she would set out a bowl of the rice with a pair of chopsticks meant for me, as we always did to show that a missing person was not forgotten. I could visualize the table as though I were actually there. This was the first birthday I had spent away from home. A year before, I had wondered, without the faintest notion, where I would be a year from that day. Now I had the answer: I was in America, working as domestic help and struggling with English.

While I toiled at Drew School, U.S.-Japan relations seemed to deteriorate further. As far as Tokyo was concerned, Washington was "adamant" in refusing to endorse Japan's China policy. A conflict within the cabinet concerning policy toward the United States in this regard had forced Prime Minister Fuminaro Konoye to resign on October 16. He was replaced by a hardliner, his own war minister—General Hideki Tojo. It had been decided at the September 6 Imperial Conference—a meeting held in the presence of the Emperor—that if there was "no prospect of having our position accepted by Washington by early October, then we must immediately decide to go to war with the United States," according to the official minutes.

By mid-October, it had become clear there was indeed no such prospect. Though the Japanese government continued negotiations with Washington, on November 5 it decided the point of no return had been reached. D-Day was to be December 7 (December 8 in Japan). The cabinet immediately dispatched Ambassador Saburo Kurusu to Washington via a Pan American clipper.

Mr. Kurusu was chosen to help Ambassador Kichisaburo Nomura, an admiral, on the basis of his familiarity with the United States and his facility with English. Mr. Kurusu's arrival in America seemed to me to bring a ray of hope to the increasingly gloomy outlook of Japan–U.S. relations.

Affected by the dark mood reflected in the newspaper headlines during these weeks, I often dreamed about being back in Japan. One night, I dreamt I was on the campus of Ono Middle School, telling myself I had come back from America but must return there to achieve what I had set out to do. I could not return home without completing my own mission. But the next class, I realized to my horror, was military training, and my hair had grown long since I had left school. I panicked because I would certainly be reprimanded by Mr. Kamio, who was a martinet. My fear of Mr. Kamio was compounded by my fear of the trouble I would have to go through to make my way back to America again—getting a passport and visa, and so forth. I saw myself falling terror-stricken through bottomless darkness. Aware that there was nothing to support my weight as my descent through the abyss accelerated, I woke up almost screaming.

The very next night I dreamed again that I was back home, speaking to my parents in the tatami-floored living room. I was happy to be back after such a long time. But my parents looked disconsolate for reasons that were a mystery to me. The dream was so realistic that I actually found myself saying, "This is not a dream. This is reality." And yet, I could not recall how I had left San Francisco or anything about what my homeward passage across the Pacific had been like. I kept trying to comprehend the sheer void in my memory about that segment of my supposed experience.

On December 4, Thursday, the newspapers announced on their front pages the arrival at Singapore of two British battleships, the *Prince of Wales* and the *Repulse*. I did not—nor did anyone else in the world—have the slightest inkling that these two dreadnoughts, the pride of the British Navy, would be sent to the bottom of the sea only a few days later.

December 6, 1941, was a Saturday. I returned to Aunt Kané's house late that night and enjoyed a bath in the wooden Japanese tub. The weather was bright and warm on the following day, Sunday. In the morning I played table tennis with some of the young Japanese employees of the nursery, who lived in a dormitory on the grounds.

While we chatted at the table after lunch, the Shimizus had the radio on. Suddenly, I saw them listening intently to a newscast which had abruptly cut into the music. I did not understand what was being reported. All I could catch was "Japanese planes" and "Pearl Harbor."

Mr. Shimizu translated for us: "Japanese planes are now bombing Pearl Harbor."

No! It can't be! There must be some mistake, I thought. But the incredible newscast continued. Many American warships had been damaged and some Japanese planes shot down. There was no mistake about what was happening. This *was* war.

The Japanese foreman, who had heard the news in his own house on the grounds, came in and joined us. He said, "I think all of us will be thrown into some camp."

As he said this, he laughed. I could see he was trying to cloak his anxiety with forced cheerfulness.

Mr. Shimizu, who was a few years older than the foreman, said, "America would not do anything unreasonable," reflecting what I thought was his faith in American democracy. Yet he, too, could not hide his apprehension.

So this was the "surprise attack" I had heard about in Japan. Some Navy officers who had been speaking before groups of civilians to make them more aware of the international situation had been saying that when war came, the Navy would "hit" Pearl Harbor and Guam before a declaration of war. This was the vaunted weapon in their strategy to ensure victory. I had heard about this but dismissed the possibility as remote, unreal, and of no concern to me. But now the Japanese Navy was living up to what it had unofficially promised.

My first reaction on December 7, in any event, was that I *had been deceived*. I had believed all along that war would be averted.

The dreaded possibility became real, however, and the undeniable verdict emerged: I was, after all, a dumb fool to have left Japan at the time I did. But only one—the foreman—would verbalize it. He used an apt proverb: *Tonde hini iru natsuno mushi*. He was comparing me to "a summer insect that seeks light and ends up being burned by fire." The proverb refers to a person who deliberately courts disaster.

I felt insulted by his remark, but I could not deny its validity. For now, I had no idea of what I should or could do under the circumstances, for which I had not prepared myself.

Back in San Francisco that night, I found the sedate city in turmoil. At each street corner, newspaper vendors were hawking extras with half-page-high headlines. At least one paper displayed a single word on page one: "WAR!"

Curious about the Japanese section of the town that roughly centered on Sutter and Fillmore Streets, I took a streetcar instead of the usual California Street cable car. As the tram swung around a corner, I caught a glimpse of a brightly-lit room in a building, in which many nurses were busily outfitting themselves for what appeared to be an emergency assignment. It was Red Cross headquarters, and I knew that the nurses were being dispatched to Pearl Harbor. The war, which for the past several hours had been only "news," suddenly took on somber aspects of reality.

In the Japanese section, most of the shops were closed and an unusual number of uniformed policemen were out—evidently to cope with any untoward incidents.

I saw a man about my age with Japanese features encounter an apparent Caucasian acquaintance of his and raise his hands to half cover his face in what I presumed was an exaggerated gesture to indicate his embarrassment. To me this was not only surprising but upsetting. Assuming he was a Nisei—there were very few Japanese nationals my age in California at the time—why should he, an American citizen, feel that way? Even I, a Japanese subject, was most certainly not responsible for the surprise attack. There was absolutely no reason why a Nisei should feel apologetic about it. I expected him to be just as angry as any other American.

After returning to the Hammonds' residence and sitting at my desk, I wondered about the day's implications. The surprise attack was evidently a great tactical success for Japan. What would happen now? An invasion of Hawaii or the West Coast? If the latter should be the case, what must I do?

The answer came naturally. I conjured up a juvenile fantasy of heroically crossing no-man's-land in order to join the Japanese forces. I felt I was duty-bound to do so. The five years of military training in middle school had taught me that anything else would be shameful.

Several years earlier, I had read a novel by Kyosuke Fukunaga, a naval officer turned writer, entitled *The Future Japan-U.S. War*. At the outset of the war, two Nisei living in or near San Francisco decide to unlock the airship *Akron* from its moorings on a warship at anchor in San Francisco Bay. They succeed in releasing the airship but are caught and summarily executed by firing squad. I knew that in the reality of December 1941 nothing like this would ever happen. According to everything I had learned in ultranationalistic Japan, the two characters in the novel were "true Japanese." But the Nisei I knew exhibited none of the behavior I had been taught to associate with heroism. I felt that even if there were Nisei who were Japanese citizens, none would have guts enough to sacrifice themselves like the "heroes" in Fukunaga's fiction.

But suppose there were no invasion? What should I do? Was it possible that I could still pursue my objective? Would it be realistic? These thoughts kept me from falling asleep for a long time that night.

The following day, Monday, I went to school full of thoughts about the impact of Sunday's event. But more than anything, my primary concern was to remain—or at least appear—unperturbed, like a true samurai in the face of adversity, and certainly not like the young Nisei I had seen the night before.

At Drew School, there were usual greetings among students but hardly a smiling face. In the second session, which began at nine o'clock, Principal Drew ordered all students and faculty to assemble in the study hall, the largest room of the building.

The usually composed and suave Mr. Drew appeared tense and irritable that morning as he addressed the gathering. I did not understand all he said but did catch the adjective "treacherous" several times—the word he used to characterize the surprise attack by the Japanese Navy. Then he turned on the radio that had been brought into the room for the occasion. We heard President Roosevelt's address to Congress and I gathered that this was designed to obtain Congressional approval of a declaration of war against Japan and Germany. Roosevelt also used the word "treacherous" to denounce Japan's surprise attack.

The class after this special session was Mr. Judge's English II. The teacher said nothing about the war but the impact it had on him was palpable: The unparalleled sense of humor with which he entertained his class—and even me—was gone. After the class I spoke briefly with him at the door. He expressed his sympathy with me over the fact that the war would now make it impossible for me to correspond with my parents in Japan, and also over my future in America. I asked about his brother, who I had been told was with the Army in Hawaii. Mr. Judge said he had indeed been concerned about him, and I realized this was the primary reason he was not his usual self during the class.

In Mr. Spitzer's American History I found the entire class more interested in the history now unfolding than in the Civil War of eighty years earlier. During discussions about war and whether or not there would be a Japanese invasion of the West Coast, one student asked about whether "Japanese saboteurs and spies" would aid the invading forces. To this, Mr. Spitzer answered that, if so, they would pose no serious problems because "just as you can see from the example in this class, they would be conspicuous."

It must be admitted that Mr. Spitzer had never been overwhelmingly friendly toward me. Nonetheless, I was annoyed by the way he referred to my presence in the class. So I decided to make a statement of my own.

I raised my hand and spoke with an eloquence that surprised me: "Americans are proud of democracy. But I think it is rather inconvenient. When an enemy has attacked, the President must obtain approval by the Congress to declare war on him."

I truly felt that the democratic process by which Congress exercised restraint on the Chief Executive did not lend itself well to coping with a national emergency.

Mr. Spitzer replied, "That is how a democracy can prevent the emergence of a dictator." His statement made the American system a little more understandable.

The newspapers of December 8 reported that the attack on Pearl Harbor the day before had begun at 7:30 A.M. local time, while the soldiers and sailors were still asleep. Casualties were reported to be about three thousand.

Another news item caught my eye. In an interview, Saburo Kido, an attorney and a leader of the Japanese-American Citizens' League, asserted that Nisei were "loyal to America" and that he wanted other Americans to believe this. The article also mentioned that persons of Japanese descent in the United States numbered 150,000, of whom seventy percent were American citizens.

I also read in the papers that on the night of December 7, the FBI had arrested a large number of Japanese in the San Francisco area who had been under surveillance as potentially dangerous aliens. These included leaders of the Japanese-American community such as the heads of the associations of Japanese from particular prefectures, the president of a branch of the nationalist group called Kokuryukai (Black Dragon Society), and high-ranking members of other organizations considered closely tied to Japan.

On the following day, as I was washing dishes after breakfast, Mr. Shimizu appeared in the Hammonds' kitchen and said I should return to San Leandro with him. As I threw my books, clothes, and other belongings into his car, Mr. Shimizu, who had come with a bouquet of roses from the nursery, told Mr. Hammond about his decision. Mr. Hammond said, "The war has nothing to do with Kiyoaki," and asked me to continue to stay there to work. But Mr. Shimizu insisted that it was better that I stayed with Aunt Kané, and we left.

I stopped over at Drew School to say goodbye to Mr. Drew first.

But Miss Fish, his secretary, said with a sneer, "Mr. Drew is busy until 10:30 every morning," meaning that I could not see him.

I went up to Mr. Judge's class and knocked on the door. As he came out and closed the door behind him, I told him I would stay away from school for the time being. Mr. Judge was very sympathetic.

"Do write me, Kiyoaki," he said. " And I will write to you."

To give me his address, he tore a lined blank page out of his notebook and held it on the door.

"All right. This is the envelope," he said, drawing a rectangle with a red pencil, and wrote his address in its center.

"And up here you put a stamp of George Washington."

He drew a face at top right with mouth, nose, and eyes represented by dots. I was relieved that Mr. Judge had not quite lost his sense of humor.

Back at San Leandro, I spent time helping with nursery work and making up bundles of roses with the Japanese employees. I also drove the Ford tractor, gaining the satisfaction of operating a motored vehicle even though I had no opportunity to drive an automobile.

Being released from homework, however, I did have much more time to think about war and my own future. Only a year or two before at Ono Middle School, I recalled, I used to wonder about war—the so-called Sino-Japanese Incident my country was fighting. At that time "war" seemed like a concept far removed from the reality of my own life. As we had been taught to accept it, war was a noble and glorious mission for our nation. The men who took part in it were loyal and dauntless heroes, devoting their lives to the state.

The first time I was told that war was a wretched thing was when I traveled to Tokyo with my prefecture's rifle team for the national athletic meet. The leader of our group, a lieutenant from another middle school, had fought in China. When I asked him with boyish naiveté, "Is war fun?" the reserve officer snapped angrily, "That's the trouble with you fellows—thinking that war is fun! War is pathetic.

. . . Some of my own men died in my arms, crying for their mothers."

It was a sobering account of war—the first I ever heard. I wanted to tell the officer that I could not be blamed for asking the question, because no one had ever told us anything bad about war. But I remained respectfully silent.

In those years I also wondered if any Japanese students were studying in China. If there was one, under what kind of tension would he be living? And how much danger would he be facing in his personal life?

Now I had a real reason to ponder these questions.

Despite the extraordinary position I found myself in, however, I still hoped to be able to throw myself into a situation where I faced death. Such an experience, I thought, would be even more valuable than the rare one I was then having in America after Pearl Harbor.

Still, apart from such a personal interest in the crucible of war, I was beginning to have another view of it. I was becoming increasingly aware that the primary effect of war was destruction, regardless of whatever poetic romanticism a human being might derive from considering it. Such a realization stemmed partly from a quotation I had read in a magazine: "There has never been a 'bad peace' or a 'good war'."

I missed Drew School. Toward the end of December, I dreamed that I was back at the school, in Mr. Judge's Room 11. Strangely enough, there were no students—except one: Ramona. Even Mr. Judge was not there. Ramona and I were seated side by side as usual, facing the blackboard. Soon I found ourselves lying down alongside each other, and the desks had turned into quilts covering us up to the neck. Ramona had turned her face toward me, and as I looked at her, I knew she expected me to act in a certain manner. I was enraptured, and yet I deliberately contradicted her anticipation and kissed her on the forehead. At the moment of my physical contact with her, I awoke.

I was able to listen to shortwave radio broadcasts from Tokyo with the big radio in the second-floor living room of my great-aunt's residence. Atmospheric conditions varied from day to day and so did the reception. Each English newscast was followed by music, which was usually the popular wartime melodies familiar to me.

One night the newscaster said that Admiral Isoroku Yamamoto, Commander-in-Chief of the Combined Fleet of the Imperial Japanese Navy, had said before Pearl Harbor that if Japan were to fight the United States, she would fight until she "dictated peace at the White House." The quotation was played up in the American press as an illustration of Japan's warmongering. After the war, however, it was found that this quotation was inaccurate. What Yamamoto had said was that if Japan were go to war with the United States, she *must be prepared to be able to* dictate peace in the White House. It was his oblique way of saying that Japan should be absolutely certain of winning if she were to decide to fight with the United States.

There was no work at the nursery on Christmas, and a young employee and I took a bus trip to Oakland to see a movie. The newsreel showed—for the first time for us—the bombing of Pearl Harbor, with columns of black smoke billowing from the wrecked warships. This footage was followed by one showing Clark Kawakami, an American employee of Japan's Domei News Agency, standing against the background of the Capitol building in Washington with his ex-actress wife hanging from his arm. A tense expression on his face, Kawakami said the surprise attack was "the blackest spot in Japanese history" and that he would volunteer for the U.S. Army to fight Japan, the country of his own father. His pretty wife, whom he had met in Japan, looked apprehensive but said nothing.

January 1, 1942, was the first New Year's day I celebrated outside Japan. This was indeed very different from any other New Year's I had experienced during the preceding eighteen years. It was so warm in California on that day that I was able to walk outside without a jacket on. Japan never got such warm weather until the end of March, after the first spring rain.

During the preceding weeks, I had seen many warplanes flying over San Leandro. On this New Year's I saw several, including the oddly shaped one with a double fuselage called the P-38. Indeed, I was in a country at war; yet, unlike in my own, there were no suggestions of rationing or shortages of goods. This was, I felt, surely America.

Toward evening I walked outside again. The sun had set, leaving a faint glow in the western sky. Over the mountains in the east, a reddish moon had risen. My parents and great-grandmother at home must be so concerned about me, I thought.

On the day before, December 31, as I washed dishes after lunch, I had suddenly begun thinking about the traditional morning customs of New Year's in Japan. I looked at my watch and it was 1:10 in the afternoon, which meant it was 6:10 in the morning of January 1 in Japan. I felt sure that my sudden thoughts of New Year's had come across the Pacific from my family, thinking and talking about me at breakfast.

In Japan, people got up early—well before sunrise—to celebrate the first day of the year. My father, sister, and brother, I knew, must have visited the nearby Shinto shrine to pay homage to the guardian deity of their hamlet.

As I thought about the anxiety my family must be having about me, I told myself that I must not fail them. I would accomplish my purpose no matter what.

On January 3, there was an air raid alert and we doused all the lights in the house and assembled in the living room. I raised the blind to look outside and noticed that, unlike the previous alert of a few weeks before, the blackout was complete this time. Not a single light was seen in the view from the window over the vegetable fields dotted with a few farmhouses, lit by the large yellowish moon over the hills on the horizon.

Aunt Kané saw me and said sharply, "Come away from the window. Your eyeglasses reflecting the outside light may look like room lights."

"How ridiculous!" I thought, but then I realized that the mental stress under which she had labored since the outbreak of the war had made her neurotic. And she was no exception. I had found most Japanese residents in more or less the same panicky state of mind in those months.

After I had been away from Drew School for about a month, the people around me decided that I should resume attending school in time for the new term starting after the holidays. This time, I was told to board at a private home in San Francisco—that of Mrs. Takao, Mrs. Shimizu's mother. It had been decided by the Shimizus and Aunt Kané that, contrary to my wishes, this arrangement was preferable to my working in an American home as before. I was finally persuaded because I realized that it might not be easy to find an employer willing to hire an enemy alien. Even Mr. Hammond probably wouldn't rehire me now.

The thought of returning to Drew School exhilarated me. I was pleased that I would be able to resume regular student life and, above all, that I would be rejoining the teachers and friends I had come to know during the preceding six months.

On January 5, 1942, I ambled to Drew School from Mrs. Takao's at 2033 Bush Street, only twelve minutes' walk away. When I was about two blocks away from the school, I had a moment of anxiety because the street seemed deserted and different from the way I remembered it. I wondered if school was really going to start that day. Then I saw Cheng, a Chinese girl I knew from the school, cross the pedestrian crossing in front of me, wearing the same split-skirt dress she used to. In front of the school I was pleased to find everything unchanged. The weatherbeaten Ford coupe that belonged to the school janitor was parked in the same spot. The few students who habitually congregated about the entrance steps, too, were there.

I went to Room 11 for English III, and Mr. Judge welcomed me back. He began talking with one hand on my shoulder: "My brother in Hawaii was safe. Oh, thank you for sending me the flowers over Christmas. I was in bed with a cold most of the holiday period. What did you do? Oh, yes, you were making bouquets of roses. About the book report assignment, you can choose anything you like."

In English II in the afternoon I found Audrey and Ramona on either side of me, looking slightly more mature than a month before. Ramona's heavy lock of black hair reminded me of my sister Masako. I had to suppress a smile when I recalled the dream I had about Ramona, of which she naturally knew nothing at all.

January 10 was a Saturday, and after one week of study at school I had planned to return to San Leandro. But on Friday night, Aunt Kané telephoned me not to come because a Japanese had been arrested for having traveled only a short distance.

So, instead, I visited the library toward the evening and found in *Time* magazine two articles about Japanese soldiers that said they were barbaric and merciless. When at home these Japanese men were different, said the article, but once at the front they became sadistic, because they realized they could not go back to their homes and their gardens, saké, and chrysanthemums.

The other article was about the two-man midget submarines of the Japanese Navy which ran aground during the Pearl Harbor attack. The body of one man was removed without difficulty. But the other had been caught in the engine section by the impact of the vessel hitting the sea bottom, making it impossible to recover it. Accordingly, the section of the engine with the body caught in it had to be cut out before the body could be properly buried. The account left me with a nameless sense of something painful and depressing. Only a few days before I had been chilled by a picture in a newspaper showing the belongings of a pilot of a Japanese plane shot down over Hawaii. My heart constricted as I made out the familiar sweets, biscuits, and pickled plums called *umeboshi*.

On Monday January 19, we had our first air raid drill at school. Shortly before noon, the bell rang out and we all evacuated classrooms to the basement. Because this was a new experience for the students, there was much excitement and noise. Some teachers unsuccessfully attempted to keep them quiet. Order was restored only when an exasperated Principal Drew shouted, with surprising force, "Silence!"

After we returned to our respective classrooms, Mr. Judge asked with a smile: "Well, how did you like the air raid drill?"

In our private conversation session, we discussed the war. In my diary for that day, I noted: "For the first time Mr. Judge wanted to know my views on the war. He is an American after all: He does not seem to have the slightest doubt about America winning."

On January 22, I bought a copy of *Liberty*, a weekly, at the corner drugstore. It carried an article entitled "Training for Murder," which described the war information Japanese children were receiving. Illustrations showed pages out of picture books, *China War Pictures and Stories of Heroism*, including one of Japanese soldiers brandishing rifles with fixed bayonets in close-quarter combat. I had read these books myself as a child.

In another issue of the same weekly I bought in early February, I found an article about Japanese atrocities in Nanking during December 1937. It said that thousands of innocent civilians were slaughtered and women raped. Some soldiers, they said, threw babies into the air and caught them with bayonets for fun. The first page of this sensationalist piece, furthermore, was covered by a composite picture of a hillock of human skulls surmounted by the Emperor of Japan in Army uniform. Another article in the magazine carried interviews conducted by an American journalist of Japanese soldiers taken prisoner in the Philippines. The article said most of the Japanese soldiers knew such simple English words as "O.K.," "Please," and "Thank you." I thought the first article was an exaggeration of facts; the other, I thought, could not be a fabrication. Despite *Senjinkun's* exhortations to Japanese fighting men never to surrender, there *were* Japanese soldiers held behind enemy lines. The single issue of the weekly magazine made me feel totally lost, as though I had been betrayed by my best friend.

Chapter 7

Goodbye, Drew School

The arrest by the FBI of "dangerous" aliens continued throughout the weeks after the Pearl Harbor attack. Some of my Japanese acquaintances said I, too, would be arrested any day because I had come to America so recently. I had no reason to doubt such a possibility. In retrospect, however, that supposition was not valid. Those placed into custody were senior residents in the Japanese community—those with influence over their fellow Japanese. But I had not lived in the United States long enough to deserve the suspicion of being important; I was not even a fully grown adult.

At the time, though, I expected to receive some sort of contact from the FBI any day. Whenever I went out in the evening to see a movie, I would tell Mrs. Takao: "If an FBI man comes after me, please tell him to leave his office address and I will go there later."

During January I heard rumors that eventually all Japanese nationals would be incarcerated and that camps were being built for that purpose. The four-o'clock radio news on January 29 quoted Francis Biddle, the attorney general, as stating that the Japanese, Germans, and Italians living in twenty-odd areas on the West Coast, such as San Francisco and Los Angeles, were to be moved to the interior within thirty days. The news made the already jittery Japanese population even more so.

I returned to San Leandro on January 31, a Saturday. During my conversation with Aunt Kané, it came out that I had failed to obey her instructions to destroy all the "dangerous," that is, incriminating, items I had in my possession. By this, she meant letters from my friends in Japan and some photographs that reflected Japanese nationalism and militarism. I knew Aunt Kané was concerned not only about my safety but about the possibility that my things would incriminate other people around me as well.

She insisted that I dispose of them. I went through my desk drawers and selected what she would consider "dangerous," namely, the Rising Sun flags and some of the letters from my friends, including one from Osamu Matsusue in which he said he was preparing for the entrance examination of the military academy. Looking at these mementos, however, I became extremely reluctant to part with them. If I were to be deemed "dangerous" because of these letters expressing genuine friendship and human concern for me, I felt, I would only be too pleased to be deprived of liberty. If I were to be imprisoned for owning a national flag of the country to which I owed my allegiance, I would be proud of the incarceration. I decided not to dispose of these items.

On February 4, all Japanese nationals were registered by the United States government as enemy aliens. The makeshift registration center I went to had been set up in Kinmon Gakuen, a school in the heart of the Japanese section of San Francisco. Japanese-American children went there after school to study the Japanese language and other subjects with the same government-edited textbooks used in primary schools in Japan.

The person who handled my registration was an attractive blonde in her twenties. After an exchange of a few words, she asked me pleasantly, "How long have you been in America?"

"I have been here for seven months."

"I thought you had been here all your life."

Perhaps she was only being kind—my English was hardly as good as that of the Nisei, who had indeed been in America all their lives. But other Japanese aliens were another story. Very few of the first-generation immigrants (Issei) on the West Coast were able to speak English. I accepted her remark as a major compliment.

After supper on the following day, the doorbell rang and I found the mailman with my Certificate of Identification, a booklet with pink covers. The mailman asked me to produce my Alien Registration Receipt Card, and then checked the photograph inside the certificate to be sure there was no mistake. The booklet carried a print of my right index finger as well as my photograph, personal data, and alien registration number (7560703). It was signed by Jeanette Livingston, the personable blonde.

The document listed the restrictions governing my travel, change of residence, occupation or employment, and possession of cameras, radios, firearms, ammunition, explosives, signal devices, and similar other articles. There were areas, such as those near military facilities, that I could not enter without official permission. Any violation of these regulations and instructions could subject me to "detention and internment for the duration of the war."

In those weeks of mounting gloom, the only happy time of my life was the noon recess, when I was able to speak with Mr. Judge. Unfortunately, the extra session of private instruction had been discontinued because Mr. Drew disapproved of it. The progress I had made in speaking English by this time was thanks largely to Mr. Judge's special attention.

One day in early February, we again discussed my reason for being in America. This time, my answer was different from that which I had given Mr. Judge shortly after meeting him. It reflected the impact of the war on me.

I said: "I want to devote my whole life to international peace by understanding the United States. Many students come from Japan to America. But very few go from America to Japan. And very few Japanese study in China. I think the Sino-Japanese war started because Japanese did not understand the Chinese. Japanese were ignorant of China."

The implication of my statement was obvious. Mr. Judge responded by saying, "All right. I will go to Japan to study as soon as the war is over. How much will it cost to live in a good home, eat good food, and go to school for a year?"

"I don't know," I said, because I really had no notion. "But one hundred dollars is worth four hundred yen." This was about four times the monthly salary my father was drawing as a primary school principal.

"Whew!" Mr. Judge whistled as was his habit. "That's terrific. I will learn Japanese from you in Japan."

On the night of February 8, the Shimizus and Aunt Kané came to visit with me and Mrs. Takao. As they were leaving, I walked them out to the car. When I closed the door for my great-aunt, she said "Just a moment!" as though she had something urgent to tell me. I opened the door again and stuck my head inside.

Aunt Kané whispered into my ear: "I'm going to burn those Rising Sun flags." She had discovered that I had not gotten rid of those "dangerous" items. She was not asking for my permission; she was merely informing me of what she intended to do.

"Burn them?" I shot back loudly.

The scene of the *Kamakura Maru* leaving the Kobe pier and the people who had come to see me off flashed through my mind. I winced at the thought of having to lose something so precious. But the next moment I nodded, indicating my consent—or resignation, rather—to Aunt Kané's intention. Amused by the expression on my face, which must have unmistakably mirrored my heartbreak, all three people in the car laughed. This made me even more miserable.

In those months of uncertainty and tension, I would occasionally give vent to my feelings in my diary about my own future and the Japanese people I lived with. The lengthy entry of February 12, 1942, reflects the attitudes that had been instilled in me by the nationalistic education I had received in Japan:

> The fall of Singapore is imminent. My parents must be
> very worried about me. I wish I could communicate with

them, but there seems to be no means at present.

Today I wish to put down my frank thoughts about the so-called ethnic Japanese living here. I don't know a better expression than "shaking in their boots" to describe the state of mind prevalent in the Japanese community in this country. It is a disgrace. Before the outbreak of the war, people in Japan had faith in the stalwartness of spirit that their compatriots in America would demonstrate if war should ever come. Japanese visitors would report, upon returning home, that they were deeply impressed with our compatriots in America. The reason is that these Japanese were pioneers who had crossed the great ocean twenty or thirty years before to establish a new life in an inhospitable land. These pioneers are now disgracing their own proud history by being so timid and shaky.

They had left home to live on alien soil. Why should they tremble at the suggestion of forced removal today? Some have wept over the possibility of having to part with their own offspring because their allegiance is different. But this is ridiculous, to say the least. Practically all the peoples of the world today are engaged in a war to defend themselves. Think of the families of the uncountable millions of soldiers all over the world. How could any people defend their own country if the parents could not bear the thought of parting with their sons?

There may be evacuation, indeed. But if the evacuees are not allowed to work, does it mean we will starve to death? Certainly not. The evacuees may not be able to live as comfortably as in normal times, but the government has already publicly pledged its own responsibility for the lives of any relocated people. The Japanese nationals should regard the duration of the war as a period of inactivity—hibernation—during which their assets would neither increase nor decrease.

What matters is guts. If we owe allegiance to Japan, we are enemies of the United States. As citizens of an enemy nation, we deserve to be moved away from areas where we would carry out our duties as subjects of the Emperor to hurt U.S. national interests. In fact, we should be grateful to the United States for being so generous. Why should we tremble, then? If the government plans to remove all Japanese from the Pacific Coast, perhaps we should even volunteer to evacuate—both for the United States and for our own safety.

On the other hand, if the same treatment were to be given the American citizens of Japanese ancestry—the rumors say that they, too, will be evacuated—it would be a crime that could never be tolerated in light of the history and Constitution of the United States.

In Japanese history there are many instances of parents and sons and brothers having had to fight each other because they had commitments to different causes. And their choice—to fight—was correct. Not allowing private feelings to make us lose sight of a cause is a Japanese trait that we must treasure. Japanese-Americans are just as pure American citizens as any other American. The Nisei must be loyal to America: it is *their* cause. In fact, their very loyalty to the United States would testify to their Japanese spirit.

I have had nothing but respect for the representatives of the organizations of Japanese-Americans since the outbreak of the war. Yet I cannot overlook some among them who show no intention of rejecting or objecting to the discriminatory treatment that is rumored to be readied for them, a policy that would beg the question of what constitutes American citizenship. These Japanese-Americans seem to acquiesce without putting up a good fight.

Accepting such an un-American definition of their citizenship and loyalties, even to the slightest degree, would be an admission of traitorous intent. They would also be overlooking the crime other Americans were about to commit. I feel that Japanese-Americans should have a firm conviction that they are the most patriotic and dedicated American citizens, ready and able to serve the great cause of being an American. Only then can they destroy all prejudices and malicious suspicions now being directed against them.

I was angry with the U.S. government on behalf of the Nisei, and this grew into a rage against the Nisei for not being angry themselves. There was, however, a legal complication that I did not address in my diary: Kibei Nisei.

The Kibei Nisei were those who, after being born in the United States, were sent to Japan to receive a Japanese education according to the wishes of their Issei parents. These Nisei evidently entered Japan as Japanese subjects because of their dual citizenships. Under Japanese nationality law based on *jus sanguinis*, a child born of Japanese subjects anywhere in the world was a Japanese subject. On the other hand, under the U.S. system of *jus loci*, any child born within U.S. territory regardless of the parents' citizenship was an American citizen. Additionally, Japanese immigrants were not permitted to be naturalized under U.S. law until after World War II, so any child born of Issei parents in the United States automatically had citizenship in both countries.

Many adult Nisei, then, had actually spent their formative years in Japan's prewar nationalistic educational system. Apparently, this was one of the reasons the U.S. government took a dubious view of the loyalty of Kibei Nisei. Regardless of individual cases, however, I believed that the legal distinction between having and not having American citizenship should be foremost. Even Nisei who had dual citizenship were nonetheless American citizens as long as they resided in the U.S. I felt the government should treat them as such, and that they should conduct themselves as such as well.

Despite the exhortations I gave other people in my diary, I was not immune to the effects of stress on myself. One evening, Aunt Kané told me I would have to destroy one more "dangerous" item— the graduation picture of Ono Middle School's class of 1941. I protested but finally agreed to destroy it on the morrow.

That night, I dreamed that I was back at home, speaking to my mother and elder sister, Akiko, who should not have been there because she had been scheduled to get married on December 14, 1941. I had expected my mother to be pleased to see me back, but she appeared curiously morose, making me unhappy. I was also sorry about having left unfinished so many things I had planned to accomplish in America.

I picked up a newspaper, eager to read the news in Japanese after so long. But I could not decipher a single character on the first page. I turned on the radio, the familiar piece of furniture in our home. Only static came out, and I was not able to discern a word.

I woke up to a sunny Saturday. The distant hills and the sky were blue. There were winds, but it was not cold. This was so different from home. Under the bright California sun, I walked with a heavy heart through the many rows of greenhouses to the boiler room situated on the edge of my great-aunt's spacious nursery. In my hand, I carried the "dangerous" photograph. It showed 172 boys and several teachers, including an officer in Army uniform who was seated center front next to the principal. In the background were our school flag and the Rising Sun flag, crossed with their poles forming an "X." The boiler room was to be its crematorium.

I opened the door of the boiler and my face reflected the orange flames of burning oil.

"Forgive me, friends and teachers!" I shouted, close to tears, as I threw the picture into the blaze. It was consumed in one brief moment. I thought then that I would never forget that day and those orange flames as long as I lived.

Two days later, February 19, 1942, President Roosevelt signed Executive Order 9066, which authorized the Secretary of War and any military commander to designate areas anywhere in the United States from which any person, citizen or alien, might be excluded.

On the morning of February 20, Mr. Shimizu came to pick me up after his usual visit to the flower market in San Francisco. We stopped over at an Oakland bakery to order a birthday cake for Aunt Kané. When Mr. Shimizu telephoned his wife, he learned that an FBI agent was waiting for him. He hung up the phone and hurriedly advised me to return alone to San Francisco instead of going home with him. Shortly before noon, I was told by phone that Mr. Shimizu had been taken away by the FBI agent for questioning. He was a member of the association of Japanese residents from Hiroshima prefecture and of the association of permanent residents in America who had been exempted from military service in Japan. The latter organization had been making monetary contributions to a number of patriotic causes in Japan to make up for their failure to fulfill their duty of serving in the armed forces.

For these affiliations, Mr. Shimizu had anticipated being questioned by the FBI sooner or later. Because of this development involving a person close to me, I began to think that my turn would come soon. The thought was not cheering, to say the least.

The following day, Sunday, I returned to San Leandro by bus and found Mrs. Shimizu looking understandably pale. Mr. Shimizu was being detained at the immigration bureau in San Francisco and there was no indication when he might be released. His two young sons had been told, "Daddy is away on a trip." The newspapers reported that a large number of Japanese in the San Francisco Bay area had been placed in custody.

On Monday, February 23, I asked Mr. Judge at school, "Did you expect me to come to school today?"

"As a matter of fact, no. When I saw the extras Saturday, I was certain that you had been taken away. I was surprised to see you this morning."

A Japanese submarine had shelled an oil refinery on the seacoast of California for the first time. This was partly responsible for a dis-

cernible change in the atmosphere at school. Mr. McGary, who was
the soul of affability, ceased to smile at me.

An officer at the Japanese YMCA telephoned me to say the
Spanish consul in San Francisco had informed the YMCA that those
wishing to be repatriated to Japan should contact the consulate. For
a second I was tempted. But then I recalled my great resolve never to
give up the pursuit of my objective.

I was seized by despair. It seemed the war had come just to inter-
fere with my plans. I had hoped to experience hardship, though, and
a part of me still felt that perhaps I was fortunate in having this
extraordinary experience of living in an enemy country.

On February 26 I read a report of an unidentified airplane that
had flown over Los Angeles at about 2:00 A.M. the day before. The
article said that a nervous air raid spotter had thought he heard the
drone of an airplane and sent out an alert. Government officials had
understandably panicked, trying to determine if it was an American
or Japanese aircraft. A congressman was quoted as having said that it
was conceivable there was a Japanese air base in a deserted area in
New Mexico or Mexico. When it was finally determined that there
had been no such aircraft, Secretary of War Henry L. Stimson praised
the air raid spotter, remarking, "It is better to be too cautious than to
be insufficiently cautious." I found all this incomprehensible as well
as humorous. Yet it was so in character: Americans seemed to be
unconcerned about the kind of details that would cause Japanese to
go insane. I was growing to like this about America.

General Tomoyuki Yamashita, the conqueror of Malaya, made the
cover of the *Time* magazine I had bought the day before.

On Saturday, February 28, I went to the El Capitan theater on
Mission Street in San Francisco to see a movie Mr. Judge had recommended—*How Green Was My Valley*, directed by John Ford. The
film did not disappoint me and I wished it could be exported to
Japan so that my friends could see it. This was the second masterpiece I had seen since coming to America, the first one having been
Frank Capra's *Meet John Doe*, starring Gary Cooper.

At the theater the *March of Time* newsreel included shots of Japanese soldiers killed in action. I expected some response—booing or jeering—from the audience, but the theater was silent.

When I left the theater it was shortly after six o'clock in the afternoon. The moon looked translucent in the pale blue evening sky. In this particular area of town I saw no Orientals, not to mention Japanese, on the street. It sharply reminded me of the fact that this country was indeed at war with my homeland. Thinking of the times on streetcars and buses when I had occasionally seen an American woman staring at me intently, I wondered again if these women's sons were fighting in the Philippines, or were held as prisoners of war in Japanese naval bases, or even killed in action.

On March 2, Lieutenant General John L. DeWitt, commanding general of the Western Defense Command of the United States Army, issued Public Proclamation No. 1, pursuant to President Roosevelt's Executive Order 9066 of February 19. The Army order established, by "military necessity," Military Areas No. 1 and 2, which covered all of the three West Coast states of Washington, Oregon, and California plus the southern half of Arizona. Of the vast tract of land, Area 1 comprised a roughly seventy-five-mile-wide strip from the coast, running through the three states north and south. The eastern side of California was Military Area 2. The proclamation said people might be excluded from Area 1 in the future, but those who voluntarily moved out of it now would not be inconvenienced by forced removal.

No explicit explanation of the significance of this was offered, but its implication was obvious. In case of a Japanese invasion, it was assumed the Japanese living in this area would aid the Japanese troops or engage in sabotage and, therefore, they must be removed.

I wrote to my great-aunt that night that I wished to go to the Midwest right away to enter a college. Otherwise, I said, I would be caught up in the evacuation of Japanese residents on the West Coast and kept in a camp for the duration of the war. I suggested that I should move east immediately—at least as far as Utah.

Three days later she phoned me to say that I should stay with her. Dejected, I listened to her hanging up the receiver before I limply replaced mine.

I couldn't understand her decision. If I followed her will, I would be placed in detention, only to waste many precious years of my life. I would much prefer returning home to fight as a soldier for my fatherland. That seemed to be much more meaningful than rotting away in the wilderness.

Mrs. Takao tried to comfort me, saying, "Your great-aunt would worry about you if you were away from her. Besides, she would miss you."

I told myself that this should not frustrate me and that I must persevere. Had I not always been successful in achieving what I had set out to achieve—so far?

With the evacuation of Japanese from the military zone now a certainty, most of the shops in the Japanese section in San Francisco were having sales. I bought a five-dollar sweater for four dollars. I also bought a small bottle of sake for Mr. Judge because he had read about a Japanese alcoholic beverage called "sahkee," as he pronounced it, and showed a keen interest in it.

In the afternoon, Mrs. Shimizu and her elder son, Hiroshi, about five years old, came to see Mrs. Takao, the boy's grandmother. I was told that Mr. Shimizu was still in detention, but Mrs. Shimizu appeared to have regained her composure; there was color in her cheeks. Hiroshi had been outfitted in a suit patterned after the U.S. Army uniform, perhaps to demonstrate the Shimizu family's allegiance to the U.S. His mother told me that the boy's clothes often inspired a friendly chat on a bus.

I took Hiroshi to Golden Gate Park and visited the Japanese Tea Garden. Since the outbreak of the war, it had been renamed "Oriental Tea Garden." Furthermore, the old Japanese woman serving tea there had been forbidden—by whoever was in a position to do so—to wear kimono. It was pathetic to see her in an ill-fitting Western dress.

As I ordered a cup of tea and talked with her, she said "in spite of these times" many visitors came to the garden. On this day I saw a particularly large number of sailors. She said the Americans who came there were all very sympathetic to Japanese and many were angry with the action the Army announced against the Japanese residents. Some of them even wept with her, she said.

In a few more months, I thought, this beautiful garden will be ruined from neglect. My heart ached as I thought about the state in which I would find it in several more years—if I should have an opportunity to visit it, that is.

During my usual lunchtime walk with Mr. Judge on March 10, we saw a newspaper headlined "Jap Atrocities!" in bold letters. The article reported a statement issued by British Foreign Secretary Anthony Eden, describing Japanese misbehavior in Hong Kong in December 1941. It was painful and disheartening to read once again about atrocities by Japanese troops. Now I had no choice but to believe the stories, especially since the Chinese boy had given me an eyewitness account. But it was also infuriating that my own fellow countrymen should be capable of these acts. I told Mr. Judge, "If I were an Army officer and my men committed such acts, I would shoot them."

On March 12, Aunt Kané told me to quit Drew School as of March 16, when my advance in tuition was to run out. This meant that I must bid farewell to Drew School after fewer than nine months. I told Mr. Judge about it and asked him to visit the tea garden with me on Saturday, March 14, as the last occasion we could go somewhere together. He agreed.

Cold rain fell that Saturday, however, much to my disappointment. Mr. Judge telephoned in the morning to say that he had a bad cold and we decided to call off our planned jaunt. Instead, I went to the Central Post Office building where federal agencies had their offices. My destination was Room 422, the office of the district attorney, where I wanted to obtain a travel permit to return to San Leandro. As I approached the reception center, a young official said,

"What do you want, colonel?" I was amused by this use of the term colonel, in which I detected a touch of humor.

More than a dozen other men, all Caucasians, were also there to seek travel permits. I learned that these were all alien Italians who were enemy aliens too, and needed permits to travel. To my surprise, they were not able to speak English well.

While I waited for my permit, I heard another official repeatedly telling the Italians that they would no longer issue travel permits that day. This appeared to mean that all enemy aliens—not just Japanese—could be forbidden to travel. But I received a permit because I was traveling from my temporary abode to my permanent address. I realized, however, that perhaps I would have been forbidden to travel to the Midwest even if I wanted to. It looked as though the Army was trying to herd all enemy aliens into confinement by first pinning them down before camps were built.

On that day I spent all the afternoon and evening hours completing the last homework assignment Mr. Judge had asked me to do.

Monday, March 16, was my last day at Drew School. Despite my resolve to remain unemotional and calm, the thought that I would never again be able to study in the school saddened me deeply. In the history class, Mr. Spitzer was openly hostile toward me. It didn't matter, I thought, because I would not be in his class again. But I understood the reason for his hostility. He must have had a strong suspicion that I was either a spy or a saboteur sent by the Japanese government. First of all, I was a "special student" at Drew School, not needing to graduate with a high school diploma; I was only studying English. Then, on December 8, when I showed up at school, I must have appeared placid—as though I had actually been expecting the surprise attack on Pearl Harbor. Still another reason may have been the fact that I stayed away from school for one month beginning December 9. Also, Mr. Spitzer's sojourn in Nationalist China probably indicated he was pro-Chinese in disposition, which automatically meant he was anti-Japanese.

Mr. Judge's English III class began at 1:00 P.M. Toward the end of the session, Mr. Judge assigned the students to some task while he started to read something on his desk. As I watched him, he appeared to be struggling not to burst out laughing, his ruddy face getting ruddier than ever. As soon as he finished reading, he told the students, "Close your books. I have something to read to you."

Silence reigned over the class.

"It's Kiyoaki's theme, entitled 'My Eight Months in an American School'!"

At that instant, the classroom became enveloped in an atmosphere reminiscent of my own primary school days when a teacher told the class he would read a story for us. To my surprise, a sense of happy anticipation of something delightful filled Room 11.

Mr. Judge began reading with his usual articulateness, unmatched by any other American I had come to know:

> One year ago this month, I left a Japanese high school with a sorrow of parting with dear friends. On the day of graduation, we wept over having to leave the school— teachers, friends, and buildings. One year after that, I must leave another school with the same sorrow.
>
> In the previous school I spent five years and in the present one a little over eight months. But as long as I remember the five years of school life, I would not forget these eight months which, in short, were a period of happiness. The school was a garden of eternal spring filled with people—teachers and friends—with a warm heart.
>
> During this period, a remarkable change occurred in me. When I came to this school for the first time, everything was strange, and I was amazed by many things. I realized that my mental preparation for "American things" was very insufficient. In the first place, boys and girls studied in the same classroom, and they seemed very innocent as though they did not know they belonged to two different sexes. Teachers and students were like friends. I looked at this lovely community with a sigh of admiration.

What astounded me most was the fact that students chewed gum in class until their teachers politely told them not to. What was even more astounding was that in one class, a student in the front row had one of his feet on the teacher's desk. He retracted his long legs only when the teacher, after some time, very politely advised him to do so.

During the first few months, I felt as though I were a rigid stake standing in a field of freely swaying grasses. But before long, this stake, too, began to sway freely. I acquired the ability to buy ice cream on my way home from school and walk down the street while eating. I smiled at the thought of how shocked my former classmates in Japan would be to see this change in me, a *kunshi*.

They cannot imagine me listening to teachers' lectures while resting my chin on my hands on the desk.

I don't know what kind of future awaits me now. Unfortunately Mars, the god of war, raised his head between my friends and me. But as long as I live, I shall remember with fondness the life I led at this school, together with the wall clock that often broke down and the green bench in the yard on which I ate my sandwiches.

Mr. Judge interrupted his reading several times to offer explanations, such as, "You see, in Japan there are separate schools for boys and girls," or to pause when the class burst into merry laughter. Afterward, one student commented, "It sounds like a masterpiece." Others seemed to agree, and I felt that the hours I had spent on it were not wasted.

Everyone said goodbye to me, and Ramona's eyes appeared moist. Mr. Judge shook my hand, saying, "Do write me, Kiyoaki."

I was able to say only "I will," because I had to choke back something strong welling in my bosom. The textbooks I got out of my locker seemed about a foot high. Mr. Drew refunded the unused part of my locker deposit with a check for one dollar and fifty-six cents, saying, "I hope you will come back here some day."

When I got on the California Street cable car, I thought of the first day I went to Drew School. Back then, I had no idea of the many things that would happen—least of all the war, which had come so suddenly and brought my stay to such a premature end. As the cable car rattled along the track, the green signboard of Drew School that stuck out toward the street became smaller and smaller in the spring sunlight.

The cable car was now climbing a hill and I could see California Street beyond Broderick down to the point where it disappeared in the woods of Presidio. And beyond them—something glistened. It was the sea, the Pacific Ocean. I hastily averted my eyes as if I had seen something I should not have.

Chapter
8

Visalia

Back in San Leandro on March 17, I felt I could give a sense of security of sorts to the family whose mainstay, Mr. Shimizu, had been taken away by the FBI. When I awoke the next day, however, I felt ill—for the first time since arriving in the United States nine months before. I had a fever of 101 degrees Fahrenheit, and decided to stay in bed, telling myself perhaps I deserved this rest.

About 5:00 P.M., as I listened to the radio in my room, the doorbell rang, followed by a conversation downstairs in English among more than one visitor and Mrs. Shimizu and my great-aunt. In the muffled voices coming through the wall, I discerned one question: "Where is K. Murata?"

K. Murata? There were two. Myself and Aunt Kané. Apparently, however, it was not my great-aunt the visitors had come to see. The footsteps ascending the staircase came to the door of my room.

Ushered in by Mrs. Shimizu, three American men entered. The leader introduced himself as from the FBI. One of the two others was a uniformed policeman from San Leandro, who apparently acted as guide for the federal agent. The third turned out to be a radio engineer.

The FBI man, well dressed and well mannered, politely asked me a number of questions:

When did you come from Japan? How much money did you bring with you? Did you serve in the Army in Japan? Why not? Do you have a firearm, or a camera, or explosives?

In the meantime, the third man turned over my bedside Philco radio, which my great-aunt had bought for me in late January. He was evidently satisfied that it was incapable of either receiving or transmitting shortwave signals.

The whole episode having lasted no more than five minutes, the federal agent said, "I hope you will get well soon, young man," and departed.

Afterwards, we discussed whether the G-Man had come to take me into custody. Mrs. Shimizu pointed out that he had maintained a discreet distance while asking me questions. "He was afraid he might catch a cold from you," she said mirthfully. She thought I was lucky to have been sick in bed on this particular day; otherwise, I might have been asked to accompany him to San Francisco for further questioning or a long detention.

What puzzled me, however, was why the FBI man had come after a K. Murata, not a Kiyoaki Murata. If they had decided to question me as a suspicious person because of my recent arrival from Japan, they must have had my full name from a list prepared by the Immigration and Naturalization Service of the same Department of Justice.

I pondered this question as I lay in bed. Soon I had the answer. In late November I had mailed about forty New Year's greeting cards to people at home. After all, these were to be the first such cards I would send from America.

Japanese liners had all but ceased to ply the Pacific since the summer. An exception was NYK's *Tatsuta Maru*, the same ship that had caused so much concern back in July. It made a special run to carry stranded passengers both ways, leaving Yokohama on October 15, arriving at San Francisco on the thirtieth, and returning to Yokohama on November 4. This was the last trans-Pacific voyage by a Japanese vessel before the war. Still, I had thought my letters could be carried by an American ship bound for Shanghai and re-routed to Japan from there.

My heart sank, therefore, when in late February 1942 I got them all back. A rubber stamp on the envelopes said: "RETURNED TO SENDER SERVICE SUSPENDED." Furthermore, the note on the slip that sealed the cut ends of the envelopes indicated they had been "examined" by censors who were identified by four-digit numbers.

These Japan-bound letters that never left the United States included one I had written to Matsusue. In his last letter to me, brought by the *Tatsuta Maru* in the preceding autumn, he had said he was making a third try at the entrance exam of the Japanese Military Academy. He was now boarding at the Tokyo home of his elder brother, a dashing Army captain I recalled having met once. "If I should fail again," he wrote, "I might end it all with my brother's pistol."

My New Year's message had admonished him against the silly thought: "Being an Army officer is not the only way to serve our country. Look at me. I am not preparing myself for a military career by studying in America. But I feel I fall behind no one in patriotism."

I decided that when my letters, whose return address was the San Leandro house and a simple "K. Murata," were censored, this particular one piqued the interest of the FBI translator. But when an agent was dispatched to the sender's address in San Leandro, he found a young man lying in bed. Face flushed with high fever, the sender looked hardly sinister and, in fact, seemed quite helpless. All circumstances negative. Case closed.

Of course, my conjecture could have been wrong but in any event the reasons I was spared a more thorough investigation did not matter. For whatever reason, the FBI in San Francisco apparently had no more interest in me because I heard nothing from them afterward.

By coincidence, that day was marked by another event that bore a far greater significance to my life in America. On March 18, 1942, President Roosevelt issued Executive Order 9102, creating a new federal agency called the War Relocation Authority (WRA). He appointed Milton Eisenhower as its director, and the brother of the general remained in the post until June, when he was replaced by

Dillon S. Myer. The WRA was empowered to implement the evacuation of Japanese from the West Coast.

During these weeks, several thousand Japanese, both aliens and citizens, had sense enough to resettle outside Military Area 2 in interior states such as Colorado, Utah, and Idaho. But we decided to migrate to Area 2, the eastern half of California. We had faith in the Army statement that those who voluntarily evacuated Area 1 at this time would not be forced to move again.

Accordingly, my great-aunt leased the nursery to an Italian in the same business, who would pay her a monthly rent. This was to sustain her—and me—financially in subsequent years.

Our destination was a small town called Visalia, seat of Tulare County. Unlike many state boundaries, the line marking the seventy-five-mile-wide strip from the coast had not been geometrically drawn; it followed the contours of counties, bodies of water, highways, and so forth, deviating widely in distance from the coast. Visalia, for instance, was about one hundred miles from the shore but it bordered closely on Area 1. My great-aunt had contacted her sister, Mrs. Kita, and asked her and her daughters to join us there with the families connected to the nursery. The Kita family lived in Salinas, near the coast and naturally in Military Area 1. Mr. Kita had been taken into custody by the FBI as a potentially "dangerous enemy alien" because he was a senior member of the Japanese community there. For temporary habitation, we found a large two-story brick building at the corner of East Center and North Garden streets.

Moving to Visalia had seemed the best bet for me under the circumstances—to avoid compulsory evacuation into government-built facilities. From Area 2, I thought, I might still be able to find my way to some college in the Midwest.

March 29 was set as the deadline for voluntary evacuation and travel permits could be obtained only up to March 26. Mrs. Takao and I left for Visalia on March 26 as an advance party for others to follow. Speeding through the scenic San Joaquin Valley for five hours, the train brought us to Visalia, where we were met by Mr. Shirasawa, a local Japanese resident who was a relative of Mrs. Takao and the Shimizus. His home in town was modest by American standards, but it was surrounded by a large green lawn.

There I was treated to an unexpected sight—a pair of immense cherry trees with their light pink blossoms in such profusion that the entire trees looked like huge cotton candies. How ironic, I thought, that I should encounter the national flower of Japan and a symbol of Bushido in my first spring on enemy soil.

On the following day, March 27, I went to the building we were to rent to begin cleaning the rooms. The first floor was a large, high-ceilinged room suitable for a store. It was, in fact, leased by a Japanese-American general store owner who had also recently arrived from San Francisco because of the Army order. We were to rent half of the second floor, which included seven bedrooms, a living room, a dining room, a kitchen, and bathrooms. Except for the fact that the staircase from the sidewalk was exceptionally long, the arrangement appeared almost too good for a temporary accommodation.

Unlike most of the place names in California, Visalia's Spanish sound is spurious. The town was named after one of the first settlers of 1852, Nathaniel Vise, probably so it would sound like the neighboring towns in the region. Its population, I was told, was about eight thousand. Being roughly one hundred miles inland, Visalia, unlike Japan or the Bay Area, had a continental climate. This meant that even in late March it was already quite hot. The average summer temperature, I heard to my horror, was 95.5 degrees Fahrenheit.

Truckloads of furniture and other household goods arrived at the corner house on the morning of March 28 ahead of the other people. The first to arrive was the party from San Leandro, including Aunt Kané, Mrs. Shimizu and her two infant sons as well as her brother, and Mr. Yutani—the nursery manager—and his family. Later in the afternoon, Aunt Kané's sister and her two daughters, aged about eighteen and twenty, arrived. All fifteen people, including three infants, who were to live there had assembled by sundown, barely making the deadline for voluntary evacuation from Military Area 1.

During the preceding week of tension and commotion within the Japanese community in California, ethnic Japanese living in certain sensitive zones within Area 1, mostly near the coast, had already begun being herded into temporary Army facilities. Compared with these people, I thought, I was extremely fortunate to have been able to move out of the prohibited zone voluntarily.

Just about the time I was settling down to a new pattern of life in Visalia, my father in Kawai Mura received a letter I had mailed in mid-September 1941. It had taken six months to reach him— probably via Shanghai. The delay was also likely to have been due to censorship before it left the United States and also after it arrived in Japan.

Since my departure from Kobe in June 1941, my father had been sporadically keeping a diary, jotting down his sentiments about his son.

On March 28, 1942, the arrival of my letter stirred him to write in his diary as if he were speaking to me:

> Japan U.S. relations steadily grew worse since that June day, and finally came the historic event of December 8. I hope that someday you will be able to read this when you come home.
>
> Of course, I am not certain if both of us can read this together. You alone may read it. Or, I alone may read it again. Needless to say, you have no idea that I am now writing like this about you. Furthermore, you may never be able to set foot on our soil again; your spirit alone may come home. But I want you to know somehow that I have been writing this diary for you as a father should do for his dear son.
>
> Every person I meet nowadays asks me, "Do you hear from your son?" and "You must really be worried."

Some—women—even weep for me.

But I always reply nonchalantly: "I think he is all right. It's possible that he is still attending school. And, in fact, he may still be enjoying those huge beefsteaks he has written me about."

That's what I tell these people. But inwardly, of course, I am really worried about you. You may be all right, but also I fear you might be in detention. In that event, I am concerned that you might do something rash.

You must not die there. You must come back at all costs and then serve our country in a splendid manner. By this I don't mean you must necessarily fight on the front. You can make an important contribution to the country with what you will have learned and gained in America.

You must come home alive! You must not die!
You must come home after making a man of yourself!

My father's concern about me was totally understandable—very little information about the welfare of aliens in America reached Japan. And to make matters worse, a rumor was spreading among my former schoolmates that I had been killed in America shortly after Pearl Harbor. The rumor had begun when the principal of our middle school, concerned about me after the attack on Pearl Harbor, commented: "It was too bad about Murata."

All he meant was that I was indeed the proverbial "summer insect flying into a flame," and that it was most unfortunate that war had broken out before I could reach my goal. When the principal was quoted as saying this, however, it was, not without reason, construed as meaning the worst fate had befallen hapless Murata. After all, the two countries were at war following Japan's provocation. This knowledge readily conjured up in the minds of my friends at home the image of vicious mobs mauling Japanese residents in America.

My younger sister, Masako, fourteen years old and in her second

year of girls' high school, was on a commuter train when she over-
heard middle school boys saying, "Murata was killed in America."
She reported this to our parents, but displayed her unfaltering faith
in my survivability by declaring, "It's ridiculous. My big brother will
never die."

By mid-April, Visalia was nearly sizzling in tropical heat. But the
surroundings were delightful. The snow-capped peaks of the Sierra
Nevadas soaring into the azure skies appeared surprisingly near,
forming a breathtaking backdrop for the sleepy little town. If I
perched myself atop the craggy heights, I thought, I might be able to
gain a glimpse, beyond the ocean, of the island country I called
home.

Some sections of the town with elegant homes were picturesque,
and the entire community seemed wrapped in sparkling springtime
greenery. The fragrances of orange and oleander blossoms wafting in
the street at dusk immersed me in a sense of romance and wellbeing.

Above all, I could not believe we were only one hundred miles
from the coast. In central California, there was not a single sign of the
tension caused by the war that had been so obvious in San Francisco
during my last weeks there. The inhabitants of Visalia were relaxed
and congenial. Strangers greeted strangers in the street. A young
woman I had never met before smiled at me and said, "Hello, there!"
during a walk through town. The community simply did not appear
to be part of a country that was waging a major war.

The fifteen-member household soon settled in to a new routine.
The elder of the two Kita girls was particularly friendly. We often
engaged in long conversations through which my English continued
to improve.

In Visalia, there were, remarkably enough, four movie houses.
Fox, the largest and best, charged an admission fee of thirty-five
cents for first-run showings while the three others, smaller and shab-
bier, only twenty-two cents for three old features. I spent hours in
these theaters learning English for the smallest fees I ever paid.

English was not the only reason I frequented these theaters, however. Because students at my middle school had been strictly forbidden to see movies under any circumstances, I had not seen a single American movie in my middle school years. But I used to listen avidly to accounts given by others, and in Visalia I jumped at the chance to see these classics for myself. My elder sister, Akiko, for instance, had raved about *The Adventures of Marco Polo*, starring Gary Cooper, with so much detail that when I saw it in Visalia I almost felt I was seeing it for a second time. Another source had been Tadashi Fujiwara. A bright but wayward lad, Fujiwara would occasionally defy the school ban to see American movies shown in his own home town. He had praised *The Hurricane*, the 1937 John Ford masterwork, which I also enjoyed in Visalia. I wished I could write to him in Shanghai to compare notes about the film.

One day in mid-April, I went to Fox Theater to see a double feature, *Roxie Hart*, a comedy starring Ginger Rogers, and *Secret Agent of Japan*. In the latter propaganda film, the fantastic plot involved Japan sending several espionage agents into the United States before starting the war. The Japanese agents undergo plastic surgery. When their bandages are removed, totally Caucasian faces emerge. The actors used in the film to play Japanese before the surgery were presumably Southern California Chinese. They spoke such atrocious Japanese that I had tremendous difficulty preventing myself from bursting into laughter, which would have ruined the film for the captivated American audience around me.

On the following day, I was in no mood to laugh. The newspapers reported that American aircraft led by Lieutenant Colonel James Doolittle had bombed Tokyo, not causing serious damage but making a symbolic effort. Yet the fact that Japan was vulnerable to aerial attack by American planes only four months after the outbreak of the war was shocking.

Just as my father was writing me his letter that could never be mailed, I was similarly expressing my sentiments about my family in Japan in my notebook. On April 26, 1942, I wrote:

1. The author's middle school kendo (Japanese swordfighting) club
(the author is at far right).

2. The passengers of the *Kamakura Maru* in June 1941 (the author is third from left in the front row).

3. Aunt Kané.

4. Working at Aunt Kané's nursery in the summer of 1941.

5. The Quadrangle Club, Chicago.

6. A residence building at the relocation center in Poston, Arizona in 1943.
The inscription is a verse from the song "Home, Sweet Home".

7. This warning and its accompanying caricature were a typical sight in wartime America.

8. The author as a Carleton College student in 1945.

9. A service of thanksgiving at the University of Chicago chapel on the occasion of Japan's surrender on August 14, 1945. (Photograph by the author)

10. Lieutenant Judge—Japan: 1945.

11. Photograph of the author after graduating from Carleton College.

12. With Aunt Kané after receiving a master's degree from the University of Chicago. (Photograph by Frank Mayer-Oakes)

All photographs are from the author's private collection.

In lieu of a letter to Mother:

Dear Mother, the person I love and respect most in the world. Mother, I hope you are well. I am at a loss how to begin this letter. What I want to tell you first of all is that I suffer from no physical discomfort and that I am able to write to you on this late spring evening under a bright electric light. Why we had to move to this place requires a great deal of explanation which I shall defer to a later date. This is a small country town halfway between San Francisco and Los Angeles.

Grandmother [meaning Aunt Kané] and I, along with a dozen other people, are now living together in a two-story brick house with seven bedrooms. We have no problems, and we lead a very peaceful, placid life.

What's happening to Japan, I wonder? What helpless grief I find in the fact that I cannot correspond with you! It's as though we were talking on the telephone when your voice was suddenly cut off. I'm still holding the receiver to my ear, Mother, waiting for a voice to come on again, waiting and waiting forever for the voices of the people I love.

What torments me more is knowing that you are worried about me. If only I were suffering now! At least that would justify your concern. But instead I live in comfort, and you are worrying for nothing. The very thought of you and others at home in anguish about me rends my heart.

I have no idea of what will become of me. But let me assure you: come what may, I will achieve my objective. And someday, when I shall see you again, I will tell you about what I write today, and we can laugh over it. Take care until that day comes.

I poured my feelings out on paper because we first and second generation Japanese in the house rarely talked about the war or our fears of what would happen next. In particular, the older ones knew very little about the war because of the language barrier. In San Leandro and Salinas they had been able to find out about world events through other members of the Japanese community, but in Visalia they had few links to the outside. Stories of the relocation centers did trickle in, however, making all of us grow concerned that the WRA would go back on its word and evacuate us as well.

Thankful that my reading ability had improved so rapidly at Drew School, I, for one, devoured every bit of news about Japan carried by the print media. I gained the impression that there were hardly any young men left in Japan any more, all able-bodied men having been drafted to meet the heavy war requirements. Many of the articles and photographs were frightening and shocking to me, particularly because pictures of dead bodies were never printed in newspapers or magazines in Japan. I was slowly growing accustomed to this gruesome practice when I saw a photograph that nearly destroyed all my good feelings about America. The picture, carried by *Newsweek* on May 23, showed two Chinese soldiers carrying the body of a Japanese after the Japanese force was "routed" in the battle of Changsha. The capless face of the dead Japanese soldier looked peaceful, as though he were asleep. His fine features reminded me of the sons of middle-class families that had gone to school with me. What shattered me was not simply that he was dead, nor the clarity of his features, but that he had been brutally strung up on ropes and was hanging from a wooden pole borne by the two Chinese.

I knew I could not blame the Chinese for disposing of bodies in such a manner. After all, the battle had been fierce. But to photograph it and, furthermore, print it in a magazine to expose to the eyes of millions! This seemed an intolerable and utterly unjustifiable crime. My anger was irrational, to be sure, and even as I was feeling it, I could imagine people laughing at me for getting so worked up over a small thing. But at that moment I cursed Americans for their barbarism.

Still, I continued to read everything I could find about Japan. On

May 28, I read in the newspapers the contents of the report Prime Minister General Hideki Tojo had given to the Imperial Diet. As of the end of April 1942, he said, Japan had lost nine thousand men since Pearl Harbor. I wondered what kind of expressions people wore on their faces as they walked through the streets? Sorrowful? Angry? And what about the supply of rice? Was it getting scarcer? What about sugar, gasoline, and rubber . . . ? Again, my heart began to ache when I was reminded that I myself lived with every creature comfort.

On June 2, 1942, the Western Defense Command announced that "all persons of Japanese ancestry" living in Military Area 2 were forbidden to travel beyond twenty-five miles and also issued an 8 P.M. curfew. What this meant was obvious. Those within Military Area 2 were, like those in Area 1, to end up in the same public facilities: War Relocation Centers. These centers were, we heard, being hastily built in the interior.

The travel ban and curfew were intended to keep us in a corral, as it were, for wholesale shipment for incarceration. The shock these particular developments gave other Japanese was tremendous. It now seemed that those of us who had voluntarily moved out of Area 1 into Area 2 had not after all done any better than those who did not move on their own. I could see that this was an act of bad faith on the part of the U.S. Army. Nonetheless, as always, I decided to act as indifferent and unperturbed as possible. To appear otherwise would be shameful.

But I must do all I can, I told myself, to elude this immense but tight dragnet now closing in on me. If I should fail, I would be held a virtual prisoner until the end of the war.

On May 2, I had sent off a letter to the Immigration and Naturalization Service in Washington, D.C., to appeal the Class 1 status I had been assigned when I was admitted to the United States. As a Class 1 student, I was not authorized to earn money for school. I had managed to pay for my room and board by working for the

Temples and the Hammonds, but if I were to get out of Military Area 2 to attend a university in the interior, I would need to be able to earn my tuition as well. Besides, I was still committed to my goal, and I wanted to minimize the financial burden on my great-aunt as much as possible.

Now, in the spring of 1942, I thought I could possibly have my student status switched from Class 1 to Class 3, under which a student was permitted to earn whatever he could. The rationale I devised for seeking reclassification seemed perfect. Because of the war and the evacuation, my sponsor had lost her source of income. As a matter of fact, she had to lease the nursery and adjacent property to a non-Japanese florist before we left San Leandro. She was now receiving only a monthly rent. To me this appeared a persuasive condition for obtaining a reclassification so that I could lawfully work my way through school.

More than a month later, on June 4, I heard from the Fresno immigration office. The long delay, I discovered, was due to the fact that the relevant papers had been sent to San Francisco, my port of entry, and then to Fresno, the immigration office nearest Visalia. The letter said I should present myself there to file a formal application for reclassification.

Though Fresno was only twenty-five miles from Visalia and about as far away from the coast, it was located just inside Area 1. Apparently, the staff of the Western Defense Command that drew the boundaries wanted to be sure that Fresno's large Japanese population would be relocated. To visit Fresno, I needed a travel permit. For that, I went to the Visalia office of the Wartime Civil Control Administration (WCCA), a newly created office of the Western Defense Command intended to handle all matters relating to evacuation.

The official in charge, one Mr. Fisher, appeared to be a man determined not to crack a smile until Hitler and Stalin had a big belly laugh together. Yet he proved a helpful civil servant. Showing copies of the letter I dispatched to Washington and the reply I received from the Fresno immigration office, I explained my need. Mr. Fisher said I should apply for a travel permit from the Provost Marshal's Office (PMO) of the Western Defense Command. (The PMO, in fact, was the overseeing office of the WCCA.) The official said I must produce copies of all relevant papers, such as the letters, in applying for a travel permit.

In those pre-Xerox years, such copies, when needed urgently, had to be manually typed.

"Can you type?" Mr. Fisher asked me.

"Yes," I said, glad I had the skill.

"I will give you some paper. Use that typewriter . . ."

When I finished the arduous task, it was noon.

"Finished? O.K. Now you write a letter to the Provost Marshal's Office, explaining the reason why you want to go to Fresno. I am going out to lunch."

Left to fend for myself, I groped my way through writing what I thought was a reasonable letter. Then I waited and waited for Mr. Fisher to return. Having had no lunch, I was famished.

He came back at 1:30 P.M., tended to some other business and then read my draft. Without saying a word, he sat down at his own typewriter and banged out a letter. Showing it to me, he said, "Is this better?"

I realized he did have a sense of humor. There was no question that his letter was better than mine.

"This is fine," I said.

Then he typed an envelope for me to the PMO. At the post office I mailed it by registered airmail.

While at Mr. Fisher's office, I also asked him for advice on what I should do to obtain permission to travel to the Midwest to go to school. He said I should write a letter seeking admission with a notarized translation of my scholastic record from Ono Middle School.

I spent the whole of the following day writing a letter to the director of admissions of William Jewell College in Liberty, Missouri, one of the colleges recommended by Dr. Yanaga at Berkeley. I mailed it by registered airmail together with the translation of my scholastic record.

The reply from the PMO arrived on June 8, and it was unequivocally negative. The PMO would not allow me to visit even a government office for legitimate business merely because it was within Military Area 1.

June 15 proved to be another blue Monday. William Jewell College replied in effect that it would not accept me. But the writer was polite; he said my letter had been lying on his desk for several days without his knowing what to do. But he did feel that since one Japanese student was already studying there, admitting me might make the number of Japanese on campus "too many."

I found this response totally understandable. Few American colleges would accept a person like me, I thought, a student who had just come from Japan. This meant all my options had been closed. There was only one course open—to go to a War Relocation Center.

A crushing sense of defeat and disgrace descended on me. Then I recalled something I had dismissed from my mind nearly a year before. When I had received the English translation of *Senjinkun* from my friend Kinsuke Nishimura in August 1941, I found no particular importance in the document because, after all, I was not a soldier—yet. But I had been aware of the theme of the moral code for Japanese fighting men since it was issued when I was in the last term of middle school: "Do not be taken prisoner."

In other words, one must kill oneself when there was no prospect of overcoming one's enemy. Now this code of conduct suddenly began to have some relevance to me because of the rising possibility of my becoming a prisoner of sorts in an enemy land.

As long as I was free to pursue my own goal, it was, I felt, like being a good soldier performing his duty. But if I were to be physically prevented from doing so . . .

I had read in the newspapers that Radio Tokyo had broadcast a statement by Premier Tojo to the effect that "the Japanese nation is prepared to fight a hundred-year war." This meant I would be buried in an Arizona desert.

What a disgraceful end to my life that would be! I had left home with an unflinching resolve not to return without accomplishing my self-imposed mission. And only a year later, I found myself on the threshold of a virtual POW camp. This I must not meekly accept. I must not be taken prisoner! In a childish fantasy spurred by moments of frustration and resentment, I said to myself: "If the United States government refuses to allow me to pursue my goal, I must escape from the War Relocation Center. Then I must go to Washington and on the White House lawn commit *seppuku* like a true samurai." That would impress President Roosevelt and perhaps a fair number of other Americans as well about how a self-respecting Japanese would behave when he was humiliated.

Of course, I did not dwell on the basic question of how I would get to Washington, not to mention obtaining the necessary implement for performing ritual suicide. But for a few minutes it seemed like the only honorable solution. After some silent agitation, I finally calmed down enough to tell myself that I was being an ignorant hothead. In fact, this was precisely what my father feared when he wrote in his diary that I might "do something rash," though of course I had no way of knowing his concern.

In a moment, I was telling myself I should never give up trying to find light in any depths of darkness I might be thrown into. I would not cease "fighting" even if I might find myself in confinement. To destroy myself would be defeat. I resolved to try to free myself from whatever form of unfreedom America would thrust on me—not by going to the White House for ritual suicide but by living up to my worthy commitment.

We all had to prepare for an eventual Army order to travel to Arizona. I got busy making crates for all of us. As I sorted out my personal effects, I came upon the folding fan my mother had given me, carrying the eight *waka* poems she had composed for me. As I read them again, I was overcome with emotion.

Luck be with you in a distant foreign land
Where I pray you will succeed in reaching your goal.

"Oh, dear Mother, am I failing you?" I cried out inwardly. "It's one year since I left you with a 'resolve harder than iron,' as we say. Yet I am still not even a college freshman. Furthermore, I am not sure if I will ever enter a college at all."

It was one of those late June days when I received a most encouraging letter—from none other than Mr. Judge!

"This is just to let you know that I have not forgotten you and that I often wish you were here during noon recess," the letter began. He presumed, correctly, that in Visalia I continued to study English. "By now, you must be freely using such slang expressions as 'ball of fire,' 'okay', and 'what's cooking?'"

Mr. Judge was very busy at that time, with the term ending and having to prepare for a batch of new students to come the following week.

He ended his letter saying he hoped to come to Visalia. "Do write to me often. I enjoy your letters though I regret I cannot reply with more alacrity."

Thus I learned a new word: "alacrity." He signed his letter "Sensei," meaning "teacher." He very much liked this Japanese word I had taught him because, as I explained, in Japan one's teacher is a teacher forever and is accorded immense reverence by all of his former pupils.

Another good letter came on July 4 from Dr. Yanaga. He wrote that the Japanese language school for the Navy where he was teaching had moved from the University of California to Denver, Colorado. Judging from his stationery, I presumed he was now quartered at the Albany Hotel. Dr. Yanaga, in his excellent Japanese handwriting, said it was best that I should go to a relocation camp now and then apply for leave to go to a college. There was a Student Relocation Committee located at Berkeley working on this, and he would inform it of my case.

"I cannot guarantee that you would be able to leave the camp immediately for school. But it is certain that you can—whether you are a citizen or not." This was a great relief to me; it meant, I thought, that the authorities had no objection to students moving to other areas of the United States since the purpose of the evacuation was to "relocate" all persons of Japanese ancestry from the West Coast. As far as I was concerned, however, the crucial requirement was to find a college that would accept me.

On July 5, in my diary, I wrote a make-believe letter to Tadashi Fujiwara:

Dear Tadashi, I suppose you have returned home from Shanghai and are lying on the *tatami* in your room, reading your favorite books. When you get tired of reading, you might from time to time think of me—your friend in this enemy land.

The heat here is becoming unbearable. Almost every night after supper, I go up to the roof of this building to cool off because we cannot step outside due to the curfew.

We are supposed to go to a detention center for enemy aliens, which is now being built in Arizona. This is most unsettling because we don't know when it will happen. I understand that there will be at least a week's notice, but I have heard that those who were sent directly from areas near the seacoast received notices of only two days— sometimes a mere twenty-four hours.

Yesterday I dreamed I was back home. To go home! This is utterly impossible for me at present. That's why I have dreams. Yet, if my willpower had been a little weaker than it really is, it could have happened. A few months after the outbreak of the war, the Spanish consulate offered an opportunity to return home by exchange ship. I admit I was tempted, to an extent. But, of course, I rejected it.

If I had accepted the offer, I'd probably be leaving New

York for Japan about this time and reaching home in early September. Coming ashore unannounced, I take the westbound train on the national railway from Tokyo with the Japanese currency I still have. At Kakogawa I transfer to the private Bantan Railway. The diesel engine train leaves the station as the driver with a white glove on his hand sounds the horn.

I get off at Kawai Nishi. Let's say it's nighttime. I walk on the pitch-dark dirt road toward my home, passing between the village office and the agricultural cooperative shop . . . when I see the long roofed wall, shielding the landscape garden of our home, even my sturdy heart might burst.

The night is sultry and Father and Mother after supper have not yet closed the sliding shutters of the house. In the living room they are talking about their son in a faraway country, not knowing what might have happened to him. They are griefstricken. It is then that I cross the threshold and announce, "Hello! It's me."

Just to imagine the impossible like this makes my heart beat faster, and the strong will that heroically challenged Fate a year ago is diminished by overwhelming nostalgia. I suppose I must send a telegram when I disembark from the exchange ship at Yokohama so that my parents would not think of me as a ghost. The cable would read: "RETURNED TODAY BY EXCHANGE SHIP COMING HOME TOMORROW."

On July 21, I received another letter from Mr. Judge, which made me even happier than the previous one. I realized he had been serious when he had written he hoped to come to Visalia. He was now due to arrive on July 25, Saturday, though he did not know what time it would be.

I waited for him all day Saturday, but he did not show up. On the following day, Sunday, there were still no signs of his being in town until I was about to pick up my chopsticks at the lunch table. The doorbell rang, and I ran down the long staircase to find a tired-looking Mr. Judge. He said he had arrived at Hanford by train at about 11:30 P.M. the night before. He got on a bus and fell fast asleep. When he was awakened by the driver, he was in Porterville, having overshot Visalia by about forty miles. He had to endure an uncomfortable bed in a local hotel where he paid two dollars. Sunday morning, he boarded a bus again for Visalia. He took a room in the town's only hotel, the Johnson, and had brunch there before coming to see me.

Mr. Judge returned to his hotel, where I met him after finishing my lunch. During his two-day sojourn in Visalia, we talked about many things—Drew School, its students, my present situation. As we waited for a bus to take him back to San Francisco, Mr. Judge seemed troubled. He was in a quandary about whether to remain at Drew School or to join the Army. I gathered he was not happy being a civilian when his country was fighting a big war. Yet it seemed it was not easy for him to make up his mind.

"I wish someone would come down from Heaven and tell me, 'You! Join the Army!'"

I was able to empathize with him. He had his own country to serve just as I had mine. But I hoped he would not become a foot soldier and fire guns. Rather, I wished he would join the intelligence service. I did not want my teacher to lose his life, nor did I wish Japanese soldiers to lose their lives at his hands—if he should be sent to the Pacific theater.

A few days after I saw Mr. Judge, the Army announced that the Japanese inhabitants of the area including Visalia were to board a train for Arizona on August 7. It appeared that Relocation Center facilities to accommodate us were at long last ready for occupancy.

I spent all day August 3 packing. On that day I received another letter from Dr. Yanaga. I had written him asking him to keep my Japanese books for me. The rumor had circulated in the Japanese community that Japanese-language books were banned in the

Relocation Centers. Dr. Yanaga wrote that he was willing to accommodate my wishes as long as the books were not ultranationalistic in tone but only literature and history.

Army trucks came to pick up our crates, including beds, refrigerators, and my desk. The heat persisted in Visalia, but I thought it hardly compared with the climate in the Arizona desert we were destined for. According to information received from Japanese who were already there, the area was visited daily by sandstorms and was crawling with coyotes and scorpions.

August 6 was also spent in packing and cleaning up. Tomorrow, I said to myself, I shall be bidding farewell to this lovely town I have grown very fond of while learning and experiencing so many things.

The cherry blossoms that had welcomed me in light pink splendor in late March had turned into deep red cherries, in such large quantities that most were allowed to fall and decay in the grass. During the spring, the peaks of the Sierra Nevadas had been covered with snow. By early August, not a speck of white was visible.

Chapter
9

Poston

The special Santa Fe train carrying Japanese evacuees from central California was due to leave Visalia at 7:00 P.M., August 7, 1942. Since furniture and other bulky belongings had been sent out by Army trucks two days earlier, the people assigned to board the train assembled with only hand luggage—a few suitcases and cartons each.

The blazing sun had waned and the station house cast a long shadow over the now-cooling asphalt plaza. Two or three white-helmeted military policemen quietly went about embarkation procedures. By the time the train began pulling out, it was 7:50 P.M. A handful of Caucasian-Americans were on hand to wave goodbye to their departing friends.

The Army's train appeared to have been put together with cars that had been idle for years at railyards (as indeed might well have been the case). The interior was shabby and dimly lit, with the appearance of having been hastily dusted. But at least there was a seat for everyone.

Our destination, Parker, Arizona, was about four hundred miles southeast—more than just an overnight journey away. Shortly after the train began moving and dusk enveloped the surroundings, I fell asleep and slept well, largely because of exhaustion from days of packing.

When I awoke, we were crossing the Mojave Desert. The parched soil was studded with hundreds of Army tents. I was told by fellow passengers that the Army was training its troops with desert bivouac for operations in North Africa to engage General Rommel's forces.

At about 11:00 A.M., August 8, the train traversed the mighty Colorado River, whose caramel-colored waters hardly seemed to be flowing. Almost as soon as we crossed the bridge, the train ground to a halt. We were at Parker.

The little Arizona town seen from the station house had a decidedly familiar look: It reminded me of the Wild West towns I had seen so often in the movies in Visalia. We were told to get off the train and remain in or around the station while we waited for transportation. The heat was nearly unbearable.

Two hours later, several olive-drab Army buses finally appeared. We boarded them to head for our new abode, the Colorado River War Relocation Center, otherwise known as Poston. It was named after a civil engineer who had unsuccessfully attempted to convert the desert into arable land.

The facilities, which had been hastily built to accommodate a total of about twenty thousand evacuees, were located within the Colorado River Indian Reservation that abutted the river. The area had earlier been inhabited by the Mojave Indians, whose main industries were fishing, hunting, and raising maize and pumpkins. By the 1940s, their population had been reduced to about eight hundred and they lived mostly on the fringes of the reservation, leaving much of the wasteland unoccupied. Thus it was a made-to-order piece of real estate, available for building emergency housing with plenty of space to spare.

The Poston War Relocation Center consisted of three units. Unit One, about seventeen miles from Parker, was the closest to civilization. It had been completed in May 1942 to accommodate the first batch of evacuees assigned to the center. The two other units were finished during the following months, Unit Three being the last to be completed. One had to travel south from Unit One for three miles to reach Unit Two and another three miles to Unit Three.

The Army buses carrying evacuees from Visalia and vicinities drove on the straight road that cut across the desert. Clouds of fine, dry particles rising from the dirt road freely assailed the passengers through the open windows. Only those in the first bus were spared the ordeal.

When the buses came to a halt, each was boarded by one of the volunteers—evacuees who had been there before us—to provide orientation. The volunteer would speak in English and then in Japanese, first expressing his sympathy for the long, uncomfortable trip we had made and then saying that the procedures of "intake"— a new word for me—would be carried out as efficiently as possible with the cooperation of the new arrivals.

The process consisted mostly of registration and assignment of living quarters. That completed, the evacuees boarded Army trucks that carried them to their respective blocks.

Each block was a group of Army camp barracks built to accommodate troops of one company. There were two rows of eight barracks in each block. Three smaller buildings stood in the space between the rows: Two were latrines with showers and one was a laundry room.

The two northernmost barracks were reserved for common use—one as a mess hall and the other for "community activities" such as recreational or religious programs. The latter also contained a section that served as the office of the block manager, whose post was held by one of the evacuees. This left fourteen barracks as living quarters.

The residential barracks were partitioned by walls into four apartments, each measuring twenty by twenty-five feet, designed to accommodate five to eight persons—usually two families.

I was assigned to Apartment 4-B, Block 326, Unit Three, which then seemed likely to be my address for the duration of the war. I shared this domicile with my great-aunt, Mrs. Kita, and Mrs. Kita's daughters. Thus, altogether five persons—two elderly women, two young women, and myself—were to share a single living space. Although privacy was conspicuously lacking, the apartment was not totally unfurnished; we found cots, straw-filled mattresses, pillows, and olive-drab Army blankets. Windows, of course, had no curtains, not to mention shutters.

The wooden structure offered only minimum security against the elements. But Poston was notorious for sandstorms, and the barracks had been at the mercy of nature since being hastily put together. Windowsills and the floor were covered with a highly visible coat of dust. Bits of lumber left by carpenters lay here and there. Nails protruded from unexpected corners.

The first thing to do was to obtain buckets and rags from the office of the block manager. Mercifully, each of the barracks was equipped with a tap at one end. After setting up the cots, I lay down to allow a sense of this new desert life to sink in.

What a place, I thought, and how distant it seemed from home. Above all, I knew my parents would not be able to imagine the kind of circumstances under which I was now living. And even if I could speak to them, I would not know what to say. Even at this stage of my uncertain odyssey, was I to assure my father and mother that their son's indomitable resolve remained totally undiminished? And would I be able to accomplish the purpose for which I left home? I was not so sure.

One of the key elements of the intake procedure was to recruit evacuees qualified for various functions so that our camp life would be run on a voluntary, self-sustaining, and autonomous basis.

All those who were willing to work were to receive appropriate pay: sixteen dollars per month for manual labor and nineteen dollars for professional, skilled, or intellectual work. Sixteen dollars, I was told, was the monthly allowance of a private in the U.S. Army.

The most essential kind of personnel for the maintenance of camp life was cook and other mess hall staff. Two days after our arrival, I found a job for which I was fully qualified—kitchen help.

My duty consisted of serving tea and water at the tables and washing dishes after meals.

Summer in Visalia, hot as it had been, was nothing compared with that of Arizona in August. The average temperature was 110 degrees Fahrenheit. In front of the large oil-burning oven in the kitchen, it rose to 140 degrees or higher, and the cook, who more than earned the nineteen-dollar professional pay, had to drink a glass of ice water every five minutes so as not to collapse.

Most men found work in one capacity or another—as garbage collector, policeman, fireman, and so forth. But those not interested in working, or who did not have qualifications for the positions available, idled their time away. Later, many of them found a pastime in fashioning simple sculptures out of pieces of mesquite tree they found in the surrounding forests.

The camp was not the prison I had expected it to be. I have since heard accounts of camps with high barbed-wire fences and rifle-bearing MPs threatening to shoot any evacuee attempting to escape. But for whatever reason, Poston Unit Three was not at all like this. At first there was a token stretch of barbed wire fence around the camp, but it was gone in a few months. And I did see one helmeted MP by a guard post. On one of the first days of my life in Poston, I chatted with a lone, black MP who appeared quite bored. I even sauntered out into the mesquite woods without his showing any sign of disapproval. Within a few days, he was no longer to be seen.

There was indeed no need for either fences or armed guards—whether against the evacuees or what subsequent defenders of the guards have termed the hostile local population. No evacuee would desire to break out. Even if one had a destination in mind, it would be suicidal to attempt to trek through the wilderness of the Colorado River Indian Reservation. As for the hostile local population, there was none, apart from coyotes, scorpions, and rattlesnakes.

As far as I could see, all the human residents of Unit Three, Poston, soon found their new life more or less satisfactory under the circumstances. For what purpose, then, would anyone consider leaving the dwelling where the United States government guaranteed them food, shelter, and clothing (with a monthly allowance of seven dollars per person)?

Despite the unbearable daytime heat, camp life was not without its redeeming features. After sundown, the temperature rapidly went down to a comfortable level. The moon would rise over the mesquite trees in a clear night sky, and the fresh air, filled with the fragrance of young foliage, more than made up for the discomfort of the day. Occasional howling by coyotes in the distance added distinctive local color to the atmosphere.

I resigned from my kitchen chores after only four days in favor of a "professional" job. As part of the program to make life more comfortable and as meaningful as possible, an adult education department had been established. Thinking that I might be able to make use of my blossoming bilingual ability, I visited its office.

There I found Mr. Shirasawa, recently of Visalia, with whose assistance we had been able to rent the brick building on East Center Street. I was instantly hired as a member of the staff of the Adult Education Department, my age—twenty—and highly inadequate educational background apparently posing no problem. One of the first things I did was to help set up English classes for the first-generation Japanese who, despite having arrived in the United States as immigrants decades earlier, had never had the opportunity to attend a language class. We prepared posters announcing the classes for distribution throughout the camp, and the response was encouraging. We were able to start our lessons on September 8, using the far side of the mess hall in the morning hours.

With competition from the kitchen, my English class was taxing on my throat, and the instruction I gave in elementary English appeared not entirely effective for my middleaged pupils, mostly women. Nonetheless, as a teacher I received a monthly wage of nineteen dollars without having to struggle with hundreds of dishes or be covered with grease, soap, and sweat. The job with a blackboard and chalk was much more comfortable.

During the months before coming to Poston, I had wondered how I would be received by the Nisei with whom I was expected to live. I presumed that they would be unfriendly, if not downright hostile, to me, because I was an enemy alien fresh from Japan—the country whose treacherous attack on the United States was, after all, responsible for their being placed in War Relocation Centers in the first place, despite the fact that they were American citizens. They had all the reasons for resenting the war Japan provoked and, by extension, me, a true subject of the Empire.

After arriving at Poston, however, I found I had been totally mistaken in making that assumption. The Nisei were unreservedly friendly toward me, nor did they show any evident signs of animosity toward Japan. Being herded together in the relocation center, they seemed to have acquired a heightened sense of ethnic cohesion and identity that superseded generations and allegiances.

Nor did I detect much hostility among the Nisei toward their own government for the forced relocation. They seemed to have accepted the extraordinary event as something that was unavoidable.

Soon after the English classes began, another group of evacuees arrived at Poston. Among them was a sixtyish man called Masami Kusunose. According to his own account, which I could neither confirm nor refute, he was a graduate of the engineering department of the Imperial University of Kyoto. As a young man, he had studied in Europe but later drifted to the United States, and he was in the Japanese community in San Francisco when war came. Immediately after his arrival, Mr. Kusunose established himself as the cultural center of camp life, as it were, starting a number of community activities, including the production of a Kabuki number. I had a great deal of respect for Mr. Kusunose, and often visited him to discuss various matters. Another achievement of his was the inauguration of a mimeographed literary magazine entitled *Mohabe* (Mojave), which carried essays, haiku, and *waka*. Editor Kusunose was good enough to carry even my low-level attempts at poetry in his magazine.

One day, Mrs. Kita received a notice that her husband was to be released from the detention center and transferred to Poston. Having heard nothing about the fate of Mr. Kita or Mr. Shimizu until then, we were all deeply relieved. Mrs. Shimizu, in particular, saw in Mr. Kita's release the increased possibility that her own husband would come to Poston as well.

Mr. Kita arrived at Poston Three one week later. When asked about the conditions of the detention center, he replied that he had been treated quite well—better, in fact, than we relocatees.

Curious about what might have befallen me if I had been sent to a detention center, I engaged Mr. Kita in conversation about the interrogations he underwent there. He told me he had been repeatedly asked if he would swear loyalty to the U.S. He had replied each time that the question was irrelevant to him because he was an alien. This impressed me. I admired him for knowing the word "irrelevant" in the first place, as well as for sticking to his position. More important, of course, was the idea that an internee could be released even after refusing to answer such a vital question.

My foremost concern continued to be the near impossibility of communicating with my family at home. As I grew accustomed to camp life, I began to see that even in Poston I was probably better off than many of my countrymen were: There was always enough to eat, clothing was warm if not fashionable, and shelter, such as it was, was certainly sufficient. If only I could inform my parents of my well-being, if not the uncertainty of my future!

In October, my wish came true. I learned that one could send a cable of not more than twenty-five words to Japan through the International Red Cross Committee. Without losing a minute, I composed a message which turned out to be twenty-four words: "We are all fine. You have nothing to worry about. Will continue my study till accomplish. Trust your son. Write to me if possible."

I deposited this message with our block manager on October 12, hoping it would reach my parents soon.

As the weeks of October and then November passed, the weather finally grew cooler. At first we found the nights to be unbearably cold, but once heaters were provided for each of the apartments within the barracks we came to find winter at Poston to be quite comfortable.

On the morning of November 15, I woke to find the quiet camp alive with whispered rumors. Something terrible had happened at Poston One, the rumors said. As the day progressed, we gradually came to understand the facts. On the previous night, a number of men had attacked a resident of Poston One, beating him with lengths of iron pipe until he was unconscious. The victim and the assailants were identified as Kibei. The victim was thought to have been informing the FBI on his fellows, considered pro-Japanese and anti-American because of their years in the Japanese educational system. That day, two Kibei were arrested and detained for questioning, and a crowd of sympathizers incited others to go on strike.

One night, residents of Poston Three held a rally to decide whether they, too, should go on a strike. I went to the rally site out of curiosity to find, to my surprise, Mr. Kusunose at the microphone on the outdoor stage. The issue at hand, he was saying, was whether or not Poston Three should go on strike in sympathy with Poston One. As the community leader, he skillfully steered the crowd away from further disorder with clever rhetoric. He said, "The right to strike is like the precious sword carried by a samurai. Because it is a precious weapon, the samurai does not unsheath it flippantly. We regard our strike right like the samurai's sword. Therefore, we will quietly watch how the situation may develop at Poston One."

The strike at Poston One lasted for one week until the detained suspects were released on November 24.

Four days later, our block manager came to my apartment with an unusual instruction. An officer from the Immigration and Naturalization Service (INS) of the Department of Justice was at Poston One, the seat of the administration of the three camps. The block manager said with a worried look that I was to report there immediately. "I have a truck ready to take you there."

Why would an officer from the INS want to see me? The block manager appeared to have no idea. And I was no less uncertain. The events at Poston One had made the relocatees concerned about a security crackdown. Though I had not been particularly worried about this, I thought the purpose of the official visit, in any case, could not be very pleasant. Perhaps they were planning to transfer me to one of the facilities for "dangerous" enemy aliens. Despite Mr. Kita's reports, I was certainly not eager for such a transfer.

The skies outside were ominously overcast as if to match my mood. I boarded the Army truck, no doubt looking grim. As the truck sped along the road, I brooded about the possibility of being transferred to South Dakota or Texas. My dreams of being released from the camp seemed even less likely to come true.

My thoughts were interrupted only when I spotted a roadrunner at the side of the dusty road. As we approached it, it abruptly dashed across, barely missing our truck, as though that had been the only moment when it could make the crossing. The excitement provided me with a welcome, though short-lived, diversion.

At Poston One, I was led to the barracks for community activities. The building appeared to be used primarily as a church—with wooden benches serving as pews. The administration had made the space available for the meeting between the immigration officer and me.

As we sat in the makeshift office, the INS man, accompanied by a female secretary with a heavy office typewriter, began: "Back in May you applied for a change of classification in your student status."

"Yes, I did," I said, not comprehending the import of the remark.

"But you couldn't come to our Fresno office because of Army policy."

"That is correct." When my request to visit Fresno was turned down, I informed the Fresno office of the INS of this, and received a letter to the effect that the office might send an official to Visalia, where I then lived, to process my application.

But before the Fresno office could do so, I was caught up in the evacuation of Japanese from the area and left Visalia in early August. Now the INS had lived up to its responsibility by sending an official to Poston from its nearest office at San Luiz, Arizona, on the Mexican border, which was about 120 miles away.

As the officer dictated a letter on my behalf and the secretary typed it, the significance of the interview sank in, and I was profoundly impressed with the methodical American bureaucracy. I myself had almost forgotten about my application for a new student classification, largely because of the evacuation. And now that I was in a camp in Arizona for an unknown period of time, whether or not I might be permitted to work while studying was not my most urgent concern.

Yet the immigration office, I realized, had not relegated my application to oblivion. I signed the typed letter and shook hands with the official. On my truck ride back to Poston Three I was in a decidedly different mood from when I had come. And my block manager was pleased to hear my report.

The adult education classes were growing in popularity. The mess hall could not accommodate the variety of classes being offered, so in December we decided to hold the classes at night in the spare barracks used as a schoolhouse for the children in the camp. During the day, grammar school and high school curricula were administered in these barracks by qualified evacuees and Caucasian teachers.

My lot as a language teacher improved even further when demand rose among the Nisei for a class in the Japanese language. Using the new, blissfully quiet classrooms, I taught two Japanese classes—intermediate and advanced—along with the advanced English class instead of the beginners' class.

My new career was extremely beneficial to me because I taught the Japanese classes in English. One difficulty was that no textbook was available, and I had to prepare hectographed teaching material by writing down arbitrary Japanese words, phrases, and sentences for each class.

The advanced English class also proved highly beneficial for my study of English. For the textbook, I chose *Reader's Digest*, which I had read off-and-on during my California days. The quality of English was good and the articles had a sufficient amount of new words for me. Preparing for my class thus helped me to expand my vocabulary. One of the timely stories I chose for reading in class was "Queens Die Proudly" by William L. White (author of *They Were Expendable*), carried in the April and May issues of 1943. It was a story of Flying Fortresses in the air battles over the Philippines, Java, and Australia.

All of my dozen or so pupils were women—of my mother's age— except a single middleaged man. They were all eager to learn English on the basis of their reading ability, which far surpassed that of the students in the beginners' class.

One of these pupils of mine was a Mrs. Kasai. The name was familiar to me from the beginning because her husband, Kenji, a stockbroker in San Francisco, was one of the several Japanese picked up on the night of December 7 by the FBI as potentially dangerous enemy aliens.

Kenji Kasai was detained, I knew, primarily because his elder brother, Juji Kasai, who had studied in America in the 1920s, had since become a member of the Diet, Japan's parliament. A few months before Pearl Harbor, he toured the United States on his way back to Japan from Europe. In San Francisco, he was invited to speak at a Commonwealth Club luncheon, during which he was said to have vigorously defended Japan's militaristic policy toward China.

With her husband away in a detention center in New Mexico, Mrs. Kasai was in Poston with her two teenage sons. She asked me to visit her apartment to talk to her sons because, she said, she wanted to show me to them as a model male Japanese. Though the reason for her invitation embarrassed me, I accepted it on several occasions.

Mrs. Kasai spoke proudly of her brother-in-law, despite the fact that her husband was in detention largely because of him. She said Juji Kasai studied at the University of Chicago and later at Harvard. I believed her when she said he was an eloquent speaker of English, but became dubious when she said he had won an oratorical contest at Chicago.

"A Japanese winning a speech contest in an American university?" I asked.

"His English is so good that if you heard him without seeing him, you would think it was an American speaking," she insisted. I still thought she was pulling my leg, or had been misled to believe in this fantastic exploit. Little did I know that I would find out more about this orator in a few months.

The students in the Japanese classes were all closer to my own age. One of the best students in the advanced class was a young woman named Aya Saita, who had a degree from the University of California. She was the most educated person in the class, including the teacher. I noted her keen responses to what I said in class and feared the level of my teaching was not quite up to her level of understanding

One day, I had to explain in English the meaning of the Japanese term *yukizumari* as "dead end" and with another word I had found in my Japanese-English dictionary, "impasse." Remembering that the dictionary labeled the word with an ideogram meaning "Buddhism," I told the class this was a Buddhist term. Then I noticed Aya cocking her head almost imperceptibly in apparent skepticism. Returning to my apartment, I consulted the dictionary again and found, to my great embarrassment, that the same ideogram stood for "French," indicating not that *yukizumari* was a Buddhist term, but that "impasse" was French.

Aya frequently came to me with questions after class, and it soon became a routine for us to talk to each other for long periods. I felt I had much to learn from conversation with her because of her many intellectual interests.

Since my Drew School days, my Confucian ideals regarding communication with the opposite sex had relaxed considerably. But my basic stance remained Confucian: no physical contact. I was proud that Aya and I could maintain an ideal, sexless friendship. Underlying this pride was, of course, the major premise that carnal desire was an evil according to Confucianism as well as Buddhism.

At about the time my new classes were getting under way, my parents received a slightly altered version of the message I had sent in October. It read: "We are all well and I shall soon complete my study. Have no anxiety. Please trust." A Japanese translation provided by the Red Cross was attached.

This meant to them that I would soon be finishing my college work when, in reality, I had not even entered a college. They were relieved but somewhat incredulous. However, in January they received the full version, including the more realistic "will continue my study till accomplish," with a Japanese translation in a very polite style.

Soon after New Year's Day, I received a letter from the INS stating that

> insofar as this Service is concerned it would be satisfactory for you to resume your studies at an approved school and accept part-time employment provided, of course, that you are permitted to do so by the authorities of the War Relocation Project.

The letter was signed by the chief of the certification branch, Immigration and Naturalization Service, U.S. Department of Justice, Philadelphia.

Thus I obtained what I had wanted—the status with which I could openly earn an income to enable myself to study. Yet the prerequisite for making use of this new status had not been met. I had still heard nothing encouraging from the Midwestern colleges I had written to from California, inquiring about admission. Though I was grateful for the new status, it appeared that I would not be able to take advantage of it unless the situation changed.

On February 1, I was surprised to receive a reply to the cable I had sent my parents.

The Japanese Red Cross Society requests the following
message to be conveyed to Kiyoaki Murata at 1034 Peralta
Avenue, San Leandro: "Thanks for cable. We are all well.
Wish you health. Itsuji."

Though a translated message, it had been unmistakably sent by
my father. As such, the short phrases became an invaluable piece of
communication, the first I had received from Japan in fifteen
months. Filled with emotion, I read it many times over as I sat on the
edge of my cot.

The brief missive from home strengthened my sense of urgency. It
had been nearly a year since Public Proclamation No. 1 had established Military Areas 1 and 2. If my great-aunt had permitted me to
go to the Midwest as I wished, I would be completing my first year of
college by then. So much time had been wasted because I had not
followed my instinct.

Time was beginning to run out. Even if I was released in two
years, I would then only have three years to complete my degree
before my draft deferment would expire, at which point I would be
forced to do my utmost to return to Japan by any available means.
Although I did understand that I would eventually be allowed to
relocate, as Dr. Yanaga had assured me and indeed as the name of
the WRA itself seemed to indicate, I had no idea when that day
would come.

Then the situation abruptly changed. In April, the War
Relocation Authority announced a new policy of allowing evacuees
to leave the camps indefinitely if they had "prospective employment"
outside. It was publicized by the *Poston Chronicle*, the
mimeographed newspaper published in the camp, as well as by word
of mouth.

This policy change was highly significant, and it still is. Very few
people today are aware that such a policy was made public in the
spring of 1943. The prevailing impression at present is that the evacuees were detained in the camps until the end of the war, and that the

only way to get out was to volunteer for the Army.

Four decades after this historic episode, the public was informed by the officials then concerned with the mass exodus of ethnic Japanese from the West Coast that the ultimate aim was to "evacuate" and not "incarcerate" them: It was to move approximately 110,000 persons to other regions of the United States. But when a few thousand voluntarily relocated themselves in the early months of 1942 to mountain states, local public opinion was aroused because it appeared the Western Defense Command regarded the hinterland as a "dumping ground" for individuals who were undesirable in the West Coast states. Hence, the voluntary relocation had to stop.

In retrospect, the War Relocation Centers indeed served the purpose of interim accommodation as halfway houses for resettlement. Unfortunately, such a perspective was not immediately made clear to the persons who were the targets of the program. To me at least the change in policy seemed to come suddenly in early 1943.

What precipitated the shift was the public awareness that such a "relocation" program was in progress. At least one newspaper report, it seems, was instrumental in swinging the official policy. An article by J. P. McEvoy in the February 7, 1943 issue of the *Baltimore Sunday Sun* argued cogently that precious manpower was being wasted when 110,000 ethnic Japanese, of whom more than 70,000 were American citizens, were being confined in camps as "guests" of the United States government.

Its condensed version, carried in the March 1943 issue of *Reader's Digest*, in fact, was eye-catchingly headlined "Our 110,000 new boarders." In it, McEvoy wrote that Uncle Sam "is feeding 110,000 [ethnic Japanese] at a cost of $50,000 a day.

"The taxpayer may wonder," he went on, "how an industrious, productive group that has $200,000,000 in property holdings and an annual agricultural production of $100,000,000 in California alone could be changed overnight into wards of the government and guests of the Treasury at a time when industry and agriculture suffer from a manpower shortage."

And the taxpayer was further informed by the writer that the War Relocation Authority "has asked for $80,000,000 to maintain them" for fiscal 1944.

I later read in a newspaper at least one article that quoted a Congressional source who seemed to be highly annoyed by the administration "pampering these Japs who produce nothing for the war effort."

Under such circumstances it was understandable that the WRA began encouraging the evacuees to either relocate themselves in the Midwest or farther east for employment or work as seasonal workers outside, while maintaining their official domiciles in the WRA camps.

I took advantage of this new "go East" wave sweeping the WRA camps in the spring of 1943 in pursuit of my own goal by shedding my involuntary status of "Uncle Sam's boarder."

In mid-April, I wrote to Mr. Kaneko, a former employee of Aunt Kané's nursery. In March 1942 Mr. Kaneko—like four thousand other ethnic Japanese family heads—chose to move out of Military Area 1 not into Area 2 as I did, but to Utah. There, he and his family had not been affected by Army orders since then. I asked Mr. Kaneko to see if he could find someone who would state he would employ me if I should present myself in Salt Lake City.

At the same time, however, I studied prospective employers on the list being prepared by the employment service at Poston—those Americans in the Midwest or the East who were willing to employ ethnic Japanese from War Relocation Centers. A substantial number were in the Chicago area. One of these, Mr. Casey, was an attorney who was looking for domestic help. Attracted by the notion of living in a metropolis in the American Midwest, I wrote to him inquiring about the position.

One evening, while I continued to wait for Mr. Kaneko or Mr. Casey to respond to my letter, Aya and I met in the mess hall and started a conversation. Because the environment was very noisy, we sought refuge in the mesquite wood outside the camp compound.

We crossed a dry creek and sat on a nearby fallen tree. As we talked, we felt a cool, comforting breeze, and heard coyotes howl in the distance.

After some time, I suggested we return to the barracks, but Aya would not agree. When I finally persuaded her, it was about 11:00 P.M. As I opened the door of my apartment, I found Aunt Kané waiting for me with a stern look on her face, as though to accuse me of a crime. When I explained that I had been talking with Miss Saita, my aunt said I should never do it again. Apparently, she was concerned that something "untoward" would develop because Miss Saita was older than I.

I had no guilty conscience but found the experience memorable. Nor did I stop talking to Aya.

I did, however, begin developing friendships with other Nisei of my age in the camp. One morning, I was chitchatting with one of my new friends outdoors when he said, "I am finished with this country for what it has done to us. This is no democracy. When the war ends, I am going back to Japan."

As of those months of 1943, what he meant by "when the war ends" was evidently "when the war ends in Japan's victory." This was not entirely surprising, and of course I found his anger completely understandable. But I was surprised by his saying "going back to Japan" because he told me he had never seen the country of his parents' origin. I wondered if he had been born with a dual nationality and now chose to ignore his American citizenship entirely. In any event, this was the first and only such outburst I heard from any of the Nisei in the camp.

Regardless of their private sentiments, the Japanese-Americans in the ten relocation centers, including Poston, were not in a sanctuary as far as wartime manpower demand was concerned. In the spring of 1943, the United States Army was apparently anxious to secure as many able-bodied men as possible. The administrator of the Poston War Relocation Center came to Unit Three to urge, as he must have done at the two other units, Nisei to join the Army. Although it was not my concern, out of curiosity I went to hear him.

Speaking from the outdoor stage, the administrator said in effect that even if Nisei in the camp did not volunteer, they would be drafted eventually and that volunteering now would be to their advantage for various reasons. As we headed back for our barracks, a Nisei of my age mumbled to himself: "I don't like the threat."

On May 3, I received a letter from Mr. Kaneko, saying he had asked a Japanese who owned a restaurant named O.K. Cafe to sign a letter that met my requirement. It was obvious that Mr. Kaneko, who had studied at a well-known college in Japan, had typed the letter himself. It had been submitted, he wrote, to the WRA office in Salt Lake City to be sent to Poston. I was delighted that Mr. Kaneko had found me a potential employer so quickly. My ultimate destination was still Chicago, but this letter would help me to achieve my first goal—release from the camp—much more quickly than an ongoing correspondence with Mr. Casey. I immediately went to the block manager's office to obtain the forms required to apply for indefinite leave.

Two days later, a wedding was performed for two evacuees. I held my advanced Japanese class as usual that evening, but attendance was very low because many of my students had been invited to the ceremony. I joked to the seven students in the room, including Aya: "I would not miss this class even on the night of my own wedding."

After the class, Aya came over to me to talk, and again we sauntered into the mesquite brush. Then, to my consternation, I heard her confession of love and even her thoughts about marrying me! I was flabbergasted and dumbfounded. I had come to America solely for the purpose of study. I had no other goal except completing my college education and returning home. The notion of my getting married now, at age 20—without even having started my college work—would be absurd. I told her that I had respected her as an intellectual superior and enjoyed my conversations with her, but marriage was not in my plans.

Aya started to weep. I was at a loss about what to do. It was nearly midnight, but she would not stop sobbing. After a while I noticed I was becoming sleepy and the temperature in the Arizona desert was dropping rapidly. Finally she agreed to walk back, and luckily this time my great-aunt did not find out what had happened.

I slept soundly that night. The following morning when I went to the mess hall I did not find Aya. Becoming concerned, I attended a psychology class that evening given by the Adult Education Department, presented by a high school teacher named Miss Barley. When I attended her class earlier, she had said she would be willing to discuss any personal psychological problems.

When I presented mine, however, even Miss Barley could not help me very much. She suggested that I should make friends with other female evacuees in order to avoid situations of the kind in which I found myself. I felt very doubtful about the advice because I had no time to associate with a number of women. After leaving Miss Barley at nearly 10:00 P.M., I returned to my apartment through a sandstorm with a heavy heart, worrying about Aya.

On May 10, I finished assembling the documents for my application for an indefinite leave, including the letter from the restaurant owner. I submitted the documents to the block manager, bracing myself for a long wait.

That night, dinner began at 4:30, earlier than usual, because a sendoff was scheduled at 5:30 for twenty young men who had volunteered for the Army, subsequent to the pep talk by the administrator.

An Army truck was assigned to each of the volunteers, who were brought to the outer stage with their families. When all were on hand, the program began. Besides rank-and-file residents, there were "official" participants: the administrator, members of the Poston Three City Council, a few leading residents, and three young women who had been picked as beauty queens the year before.

Each volunteer mounted the platform to receive from the queens a lei made of red, blue, and yellow paper, to the applause of the audience. The men were followed by a female relative—mother, sister, or wife—who received a red artificial rose as a boutonnière. When this was over, the participants in the ceremony sang "Auld Lang Syne."

Then came the last part of the rite. "Let's give the fellows a big hand!" shouted the master of ceremonies. And there was applause and hoorays as though the volunteers were participants in an athletic event. The twenty trucks rolled away with the men and their families to Unit One for departure for the outside world.

I was struck by how different this was from Japan. There was no suggestion of grim heroism and self-sacrifice despite the fact that joining the army in war meant the strong possibility of death. Nor was there any hint that the young men had become "heroes" to fight for their country or for "saving democracy against the tyranny of Nazism and Japanese militarism" at the possible expense of their lives. It seemed everyone thought he was coming back alive.

I recalled that at home, a young man "called to colors" attended a ceremony at the Shinto shrine held by the residents of his hamlet. All wished him "a long, lasting military fortune," meaning survival in battle. But this was a mere wish, against the greater odds of a soldier not returning home alive. He was sent off with three shouts of "*Banzai!*" (Long live!) Applause would be inappropriate, too, for such a solemn occasion.

To my surprise, my application for indefinite leave was approved only two days later. The fact that my request was granted so quickly was solid evidence of the policy of the WRA of that time: to let the evacuees leave the camps with utmost alacrity as long as they had a prospect for employment outside. In fact, it made a good deal of sense for the WRA to empty and fold up the camps as promptly as was feasible. As the Japanese saying goes, anything worth doing at all must be done promptly, I thought, and I decided to leave on May 17.

I busied myself bidding farewell to my friends and students. One of the Unit Three residents I called on was a Mr. Komatsubara, whose wife was in my advanced English class. When I told him of my plan, he was astonished.

"Why do you want to leave?"

Amused by his reaction, I explained that I could not afford to dawdle in the desert. I had a mission to perform.

"But it's dangerous to go out now," insisted Mr. Komatsubara. "This is the best place because it's safe. Besides, I don't think there is any college that would accept you. Furthermore, you can imagine how popular sentiment will turn when Japan starts bombing the mainland."

Japanese planes bombing Chicago, for instance? I almost laughed at the innocence of this man who was at least twenty years older than I.

"I have no fear," I said in all sincerity. On the basis of my contacts with Americans prior to the evacuation, I could not anticipate any unpleasantness, much less danger, in living among them.

May 15, a Saturday, was my last day of work as a teacher. In the morning I announced my imminent departure to my advanced English class. My pupils—all about twenty years my senior—found the news shocking. Some of them seemed to feel I was deserting them, probably because they had assumed I would be teaching them as long as they were there. In any event, the members of the class asked me to meet them again at 2:00 P.M.

All of the fourteen pupils were there when I returned in the afternoon. Plain wooden desks had been placed together to serve as a central table for a modest party. On the table stood two cans—vases for flowers obtained from gardens planted by evacuees around their tarpaper-covered barracks.

As I sat down, Mrs. Yamanaka stepped forward carrying a tray with a white envelope on it. Representing the class probably because of her seniority, she delivered a brief farewell address, overcome with emotion. Then she presented me with an envelope that contained fifteen dollars.

I was leaving a class for the second time in little over a year. But this time it was a class I was teaching, in which the students were mostly women of my mother's age. My studious pupils seemed to have enjoyed their studies, but I felt I owed them a debt, for I had been able to learn a great deal myself. I thought of the hundreds of new words I had looked up in the brand-new 1942 edition of the big Webster's I had been able to purchase by mail order. I became somewhat wistful when I thought that perhaps I would not see any of these kind pupils again.

My evening class for intermediate Japanese that day was also the last session. I cut the lesson short and announced I was leaving Poston in two days. No surprise registered on the faces of my pupils, because they had heard about my plan from their mothers, some of whom were students in my advanced English class.

I distributed small pieces of onionskin paper among the fourteen girls and six boys, asking them to write down their thoughts. Kimiko Yoshimura, one of Unit Three's beauty queens, who had taken part in the sendoff ceremony for Army volunteers several days earlier, rose to present me with a going-away gift of two white dress shirts from the class.

The messages all expressed their thanks for my lessons and wished me luck. Nearly half a century later, the now-yellowed sheets are still my precious possessions.

I spent the day and night of Sunday, May 16, saying goodbye to more people. Mr. Kusunose came to my apartment with a gift of five dollars. I did my packing until nearly one o'clock in the morning of May 17. After a nap, I got up at about 3:00 A.M. I walked toward the truck depot through darkness moderated only by starlight. I noticed the figures of four women ahead of me. When I reached the truck depot I found they were the four senior members of my advanced English class.

At the depot, two young women emerged from behind the truck. Aya had come with the other top student from the advanced Japanese class, Toshiko Shiraki. I took their small hands to thank them for their kindness, taking care not to show my emotions.

The time for departure came, and I mounted the platform of the truck that would take me back to Parker, the railway station where we had arrived not so long ago. Several Nisei were also going to

Parker and beyond as temporary farm workers under the WRA policy of encouraging people to leave the camps even for short terms.

At last it was time for me to bid farewell to my well-wishers—and to Poston, where I had spent nearly nine months. I knew I would neither see the mesquite trees nor hear the howlings of coyotes again.

Predominant in my mind was the thought that two years after having left Kawai Mura in central Japan, I was leaving for America once again. I knew this time I was better prepared for the journey.

Chapter
10

Chicago

The Army truck sped through the Mojave Desert in the early dawn. After an hour's ride, we arrived at Parker. The freight cars I had seen nine months earlier on that hot August day were still on the same siding with their rusty steel wheels.

The skies over the desert became light at about six o'clock without a speck of cloud. Unlike Poston, the ground here was a treeless expanse dotted by cacti. A craggy outline of lofty peaks, which I presumed were the southern edge of the Rockies, emerged against the reddening heavens.

At the station, I discovered that one of the Nisei boarding the same 6:40 train was Misao Oda, a student in my advanced Japanese class. She was bound for Phoenix to work. As we sat in the same compartment, Misao produced a package that Mrs. Shiraki and her daughter, Toshiko, had asked her to hand me on the train. The heftiness of the package gave away its contents. It was rolled sushi, a delicacy that Mrs. Shiraki and her daughter had spent the whole previous night preparing for me.

The train reached Wickenburg at 10:00 A.M., and several Nisei men disembarked there with me. My itinerary was to take a Greyhound bus from there on a twenty-four-hour ride to Salt Lake City. But there was only one such bus a day, leaving Wickenburg at 6:45 P.M. I had nearly eight hours to kill.

Because the other young men were to take the same bus for their destinations, I proposed what I thought was the most sensible way of spending the hours: to rent rooms at the motel I had spotted in the center of town. I was surprised to find only one of them agreed. The others said they would avoid contact with *hakujin* (whites) and wait out the eight hours on the dry riverbed under the highway on the fringe of the town.

The Nisei who agreed to my suggestion was named Ichiro Okada. I had met him for the first time on this trip. He and I went to the building that carried a motel sign. It was a general store managed by a middleaged Caucasian, who led us to his motel behind the store. We told him we had just come out of Poston by train from Parker.

"I hear things are pretty rough out there," the motel man said. He was referring to the disturbance that had occurred at Poston One in the autumn of 1942. I recalled the sensational reports in the newspapers during those weeks.

"Newspaper stories exaggerate things," Ichiro explained.

"I guess so," agreed the motel owner.

As he unlocked the door of the room we were to occupy, he said with a smile, "I have been to Japan—for a short visit."

We were back in civilization. After a shower we slept on a real bed with crisp white linens, not a pallet. We awoke at 6:00 P.M., shaved, dressed, and left the motel after paying five dollars between us. It was the highest value I have received for two dollars and fifty cents in all my life.

The other young men who had spent a full day under the bridge had understandably wilted in the heat. They were incredulous about our having been able to rent a motel room and were duly envious as well.

The ride on the Greyhound was comfortable and smooth, as the sleek vehicle effortlessly climbed the Rockies. At about 10:00 P.M. the bus stopped at a small Arizona town called Prescott. The sodium-vapor lamps illuminating the streets of the quiet little community drove home to me that the America I had left behind in August 1942 had remained intact. Indeed, I was back in that America again.

At midnight the bus stopped at a diner in Flagstaff, Arizona, a town with an elevation of 7,000 feet, for a snack. Ichiro and I sat with an American passenger at the counter for a hamburger and coffee. With customary American friendliness, he asked us where we were from. We told him we had just been released from a relocation center. He was curious about the relocation, and listened to our accounts with interest.

"This is where I get off to take a bus for Denver," he said, shaking hands with us. He insisted on paying for both Ichiro and me. "Good luck to you."

Toward the evening of May 18, Tuesday, the bus arrived at Salt Lake City, where I was met by Mr. Kaneko and his family, who lived in a tree-lined residential section of the city. I was pleasantly surprised that the Kanekos lived in such a good neighborhood. I thought he was smart to have left Military Area 1 immediately for Salt Lake City instead of trusting the Army's word about Military Area 2 as we had. A graduate of the prestigious Tokyo College of Commerce (today's Hitotsubashi University), Mr. Kaneko was a rare person among the West Coast Japanese immigrants. He had been able to move fast because of his educational background and facility with English.

One of the first things I did while being a guest of the Kanekos was to pay a visit to the O.K. Cafe to thank its proprietor for serving as my "prospective employer." I knew he had no need to hire me. I presented him with a carton of Lucky Strikes to show my appreciation.

Now I was ready to go to Chicago. Mr. Casey's last reply had failed to reach me before my departure from the camp, but I had his address. On May 27, Thursday, I called at the branch office of the WRA, which had been recently set up to help resettlement of evacuees. In the office I found a single official—a very lanky young man.

"I came from Poston," I said. "But it seems there are too many Japanese here. May I go to Chicago?" In those years, all concerned, including WRA officials, felt that Japanese should not congregate in conspicuous numbers to avoid becoming an identifiable target of prejudice. I knew that my abrupt request would certainly be granted because of Chicago's larger population and better employment opportunities.

"Can you find a job there?" the official asked casually, indicating that he did not really care one way or the other.

"I think so," I said, with Mr. Casey in mind.

"Go ahead," the official said as casually. No other authorization was necessary.

I decided to leave for Chicago the same evening and purchased a train ticket for thirty-six dollars with money saved during my nine months at Poston.

The seven-o'clock train I boarded was nearly full, but a porter guided me to a seat next to a large black woman, a very friendly person who soon began talking to me. Unfortunately her strange (to my ears) English pronunciation was beyond me. Sixty percent of the passengers in the car were soldiers, most of them air corps men, making much noise, drinking beer and playing harmonicas. Despite the noise and the heat I fell asleep, and so did my neighbor. Practically buried beneath her voluminous body, I slept soundly.

In the morning I saw from the window vast sugar beet fields tended by farmers, most of whom looked Japanese. I presumed these included evacuees who were out on temporary leaves as seasonal workers.

The train arrived in Denver shortly after two in the afternoon. At five, I boarded the *City of Denver*, a streamlined express train bound for Chicago. Not knowing that all seats were reserved, I had made no reservation, but a porter found me a seat. My neighbor was a thirtyish man with burn scars on his face.

"Going to Chicago?" I asked, to strike up a conversation. He introduced himself as Mr. Bigelow and said he was returning to New York after a vacation at a hot spring in Colorado. When I told him I had come from Japan as a student two years before, Mr. Bigelow said he had been a tourist in Japan for two summer months in 1939, visiting such places as Tokyo, Yokohama, Kobe, Kamakura, and Nikko.

"Japan is the most beautiful country in the world, except perhaps India, and people are so kind and friendly," he raved. "Oh, I love Japan. As soon as the war is over, I want to go back there again.

"I enjoyed sukiyaki and ate a lot of watermelon for dessert," he continued. "One thing I liked about traveling in Japan is that you can change into kimono on the train and wear those wooden clogs. What do you call them? *Geta*? And then you can really relax." The picture of an American changing into a cotton kimono on a train shocked me, but I supposed he had simply followed what one Japanese did, thinking it was the custom.

Mr. Bigelow turned his attention to a copy of *American* magazine I had purchased. The magazine carried an article by an Argentine diplomat who had just returned to his country after living in post–Pearl Harbor Japan. The writer described harassment by Japanese authorities, especially the *tokko* (special) police who, among other things, conducted surveillance of foreigners. In one instance, the Latin American diplomat wrote, he narrowly escaped a police attempt to kill him; he had gotten away with symptoms of food poisoning.

Mr. Bigelow thumbed through the article and rejected it out of hand as anti-Japanese propaganda, which, of course, was abundant in the American mass media in those years. The account of the alleged murder try he labeled as "ridiculous."

I asked him if he had any problem with the language, which he said he did not speak.

"No. For one thing, you know where you are by looking at your watch and the timetable because Japanese trains are so punctual.

"If only one half of the American population had been to Japan even for a month and learned what a lovely country Japan is and how nice the people are, there would not have been this war."

He volunteered to explain the scars on his face. He said he was a "liaison officer"—the first time I heard the term—in the Army Air

Corps, and one day in November 1942 he was aboard a bomber on a mission to Kiska in the Aleutians. When his aircraft was returning to its base in Alaska, a Japanese fighter materialized out of the clouds and started firing. One bullet hit the engine of the bomber, which nonetheless managed to reach the base. At the instant of landing, however, the plane caught fire.

Mr. Bigelow also endeavored to enlighten me about American people. "The farther west you go, the more friendly people are," he said. His explanation I found intriguing: During the process of westward expansion, Americans developed the habit of making friends with strangers in order to cope with common dangers such as wild animals, Indians, and the elements.

"So," he said, "I don't think you will get any better treatment when you go to Chicago."

The *City of Denver* arrived at my destination no less punctually than Japanese trains at 10:40 A.M. the next day.

From the Dearborn Street station, I took a cab to a hostel on the West Side run by a Christian organization for evacuees coming out to Chicago. The facility, however, was filled with recent arrivals from the camps and I was referred to a nearby YMCA, where I unpacked.

The following day, May 30, was a Sunday. There was nothing I could do except to get myself acquainted with this Midwestern metropolis, in which I had not a single friend.

I visited Grant Park downtown. I was strolling near a large fountain when I heard someone say "Hello!" The voice came from somewhere below me. It turned out to be from a little girl of about five, looking up at me.

"Do you have a little sister?" the charming blonde inquired.

The question stumped me because it was totally unexpected. I composed myself after a few moments and replied, "Well . . . yes. But why do you ask?"

"Because I want to play with her."

Apparently, her grandmother was among the elderly people sitting on benches in the vicinity. But there were no other toddlers in sight and she clearly lacked for companionship.

"But . . . ," I said, much as I hated to disappoint the little girl, "she doesn't live here." Indeed, my sister, by now in her early teens, lived about six thousand miles away, separated not merely by the distance but also by a war. But what a wonderful welcome this is, I thought, for a stranger in town.

A few days later, I realized that I needed a haircut. The moment I sat down in a chair in a West Side barber shop, the man with a pair of scissors asked if I was a Mexican—or perhaps a Filipino—obviously because of my black hair and Mojave Desert tan.

I told the barber what I was, and the man intoned with a mixture of awe and intense curiosity, "You are the first Jap I work on in my life!"

From his accent, I presumed he was Italian.

Contrary to the impression Mr. Bigelow gave me, Chicagoans, too, appeared to be quite friendly. Late one night during that first week, I walked up to a hamburger stand and sat next to a young Caucasian at the counter. He turned to me and said, "You are Japanese, aren't you?"

"Yes."

"A Nisei from the West Coast?"

Apparently he was aware of the recent influx of ethnic Japanese—ex-evacuees—into town.

"No," I stressed. "I am not American-born. I came from Japan two years ago to study."

"I am a Russian Nisei," the young man said, to indicate that his parents had come from Russia.

"But how did you guess I was Japanese?"

"Because I have seen some Japanese before." While in military service, he said, he had escorted five Japanese POWs from Pearl Harbor to a camp in New Mexico. These were pilots who had been shot down at the time of the attack. So, it was true what I had read: There were prisoners taken among the Japanese Navy pilots who were downed in Hawaii.

On June 3, my first Thursday in Chicago, I called at Mr. Casey's office, which was in a skyscraper on South LaSalle Street, not far from the Board of Trade building. He welcomed me heartily. Mr. Casey's plan was that I would attend Northwestern University in Evanston, only a few miles away from his residence in Glencoe.

On the next day, following Mr. Casey's instructions, I visited the Northwestern campus. The director of admissions received me in her office. When I expressed my desire to matriculate, she was very apologetic.

"I am terribly sorry, but we are not allowed to accept alien Japanese students."

There was a Navy order, and the reason for that was a secret military research program in progress on the campus. This was true with all the major universities in the Midwest region, she added.

That finished my business. But the university officer engaged me in conversation for nearly an hour, speaking of war—and "peace to be won."

"What is important about the war," she observed, "is that we emerge as friends. We must preserve Japanese culture." Before I left her, she said: "The minute the Navy lifts the ban, we will let you know and will be glad to have you."

When I reported back to Mr. Casey, he suggested I find out about the University of Chicago. He thought I could still work at his home while attending this university. On the morning of June 5, I went to the University of Chicago and learned that it had no summer term.

Immediately, I returned downtown and visited the Central YMCA College. The counselor at the YMCA where I stayed had recommended this school when I told him about Northwestern. The college was located in a building adjacent to the one that housed Mr. Casey's office. I was told that the summer term began on June 21.

Occupying three floors in a slender downtown building, the Central YMCA College was an unusual American college because it had no campus. But I could not complain. It was a fully accredited college, according to its brochure, which meant its credits were transferable to other schools. But the question was whether it would accept me. Unlike the large universities, it probably had no ongoing secret military research project. But judging from the experience I had with Midwestern colleges through correspondence from San Leandro and Poston, I could not afford optimism.

On June 14, a Monday, I walked into the registrar's office and said, "I would like to register for the summer term."

"Fine," the registrar said. "Please fill out those forms." He pointed to piles of paper on a desk nearby and showed no further interest in me as he returned to his desk work.

I filled out the forms and handed them to him. The officer asked no questions except, as a formality, if I could submit a document to prove I had finished high school. I told him that my high school was in Japan and that my scholastic record from it was in a trunk I had shipped from Poston that had not yet arrived. The registrar said I could bring it when I received my trunk.

Having paid the tuition at the cashier's window for three courses for the summer term, I was at long last an American college student—two years after entering the United States.

The Central YMCA College was too far from Mr. Casey's house to commute, so I set about making use of the new student classification that enabled me to become gainfully employed in a position other than that of household help. Even though my great-aunt was willing to pay my tuition, I wanted to earn at least my own room and board.

The placement service at the college said there was a job for a busboy at the YMCA Hotel on South Wabash Avenue. I moved to the hotel from the YMCA on the West Side. It was not far from the college, and besides, my employment there entitled me to a reduction of the room rate to $6.50 a week.

My work at the hotel coffee shop began at 2:00 P.M., June 16. I placed used utensils in rectangular stainless steel bus pans, put about ten of the pans on a pushcart and rolled it to the dishwasher's room at a corner of the kitchen. The other workers were black teenage girls who seemed to find my presence a novelty. They were very jovial and friendly despite our different backgrounds.

On the first day, I worked until 9:00 P.M.; on the second day, June 17, from 5:00 P.M. to 9:00 P.M.; and the next day till 11:00 P.M. By the fourth day, fatigue from the strenuous work was beginning to tell on me. On top of this I had a sore throat and coughed constantly. In a moment of weakness, I pondered quitting, if only to save up mental and physical stamina for launching myself on my college career. But was this not precisely what I had come to America in search of—subjecting myself to hardship while receiving a college education?

I was in a quandary. But it was resolved by a fortuitous happening. On the fourth day of my job, in the evening, I was energetically pushing the cart, fully laden with pans of dishes. Because of my careless loading, one protruded slightly from the elevated edge at the top of the cart. A front wheel hit something on the kitchen floor. The pan that was jutting out tumbled to the floor, and in a resounding crash scores of goblets and Coca-Cola glasses scattered in smithereens. I stood dazed, not knowing what to do at first. Then I saw something incredible happen.

My co-workers, the teenagers, brought brooms and dustpans and began sweeping the floor without saying a word. No rebuke, no jeering. The supervisor who had hired me a few days before, too, said nothing. If I had done anything like that in a Japanese workplace in those years, I would have been harshly berated by my superiors.

When I reported back to the coffee shop on the following Monday, June 21, I met my superior and offered to resign, explaining that I could not pay for the damage I had caused. My offer was accepted, and I received, on July 5, a check for $8.78 for my work of fifteen and a half hours—with no deduction for the mishap.

On the same day I received a letter from Mr. Judge along with those from several of my former pupils at Poston. Mr. Judge had volunteered for the Army, I discovered, and was now studying "an extremely difficult foreign language," called Japanese, as a cadet at the University of Michigan. He wrote that he hoped to come to Chicago to see me on his next leave.

Although I had decided not to work for Mr. Casey, I would drop in his office from time to time to chat with him. Whenever I did so, Mr. Casey was totally generous with his expensive lawyer's time, dispensing precious knowledge about America.

One day, he described for me his view of the various minority groups in the United States: the Irish (the group he identified himself with), Poles, Germans, Catholics, and Jews. The meaning of the word "minority" has changed since then; Mr. Casey, like many Americans of that time, did not classify non-Caucasian groups as minorities.

In any case, I was ignorant about these categories. I had learned something about anti-Semitism and persecution of Jews by the Nazis only after arriving in the United States. I saw students' graffiti on the wooden desks at Drew School condemning Nazis for their massacre of Jews. And the French refugee boy gave me a mock Nazi salute. As a teenager in prewar Japan I had read a little anti-Semitic literature based primarily on the Nazi theory about the Protocols of the Elders of Zion and the alleged Jewish plot to conquer the world.

In California, among the Japanese immigrants and their children, I had become aware of a strong prejudice against Jewish people. I was rather surprised by the clear indications of prejudice because the Japanese groups were complaining of being victims of prejudice themselves. If anything, it seemed to me that they should be more sympathetic to other victims. Glad of the opportunity to have this phenomenon explained, I asked Mr. Casey why there was a strong prejudice against Jews even in America.

"It's because they are stingy," he replied. "But when they want to spend money, they splurge. They can be extravagant too." He also told me that they did not like to be referred to as Jews to their faces.

Just as Mr. Casey was giving me such a candid lecture, a man in his early forties, and short by American standards, walked in. He was obviously one of Mr. Casey's clients.

The lawyer introduced us, saying, "This is Mr. Schwartz," and "This is Kiyoaki Murata from Japan."

Then he added nonchalantly, "Mr. Schwartz is a Jew," as if to say,

"Here is a living example of one of the groups of people I was telling you about."

I glanced at Mr. Schwartz to see if he was displeased by Mr. Casey's reference to his ethnic background. But he showed no response. Instead, he glowered at me and said, "I knew a Jap. His name was George Kasai."

I knew instantly that the man Mr. Schwartz knew as George Kasai was Juji Kasai, whose brother was arrested by the FBI on account of his allegedly jingoistic views and whose sister-in-law was in my advanced English class at Poston.

"He was an arrogant bastard," Mr. Schwartz continued. "But he was a damned good speaker. In an oratorical contest at the University of Chicago about twenty years ago, he beat me. I placed second."

What a small world! Now I had to believe Mrs. Kasai's story about her brother-in-law. There could be no more reliable witness than Mr. Schwartz.

He went on to discuss Japan and her foreign policy, finishing up with a condemnation of all totalitarian governments and praise for American individualism. During his forensic effort, he seemed to have gone back to his university days, his clenched fist cutting through the air. Then he left after a handshake.

Mr. Casey probably thought, wrongly, that I was upset by Mr. Schwartz's peroration and said somewhat apologetically, "He was a little drunk." Far from being upset, I was amused by the whole discussion.

Then Mr. Casey, who had not interrupted Mr. Schwartz, surprised me by saying he believed that the war now being fought between the United States and Japan was not something Japan started. "President Roosevelt provoked Japan into it," he said. I realized then that Mr. Casey, a staunch Republican, neither admired nor liked the incumbent American President. He told me, to my astonishment, that Mr. Roosevelt was always in a wheelchair.

"He is paralyzed from the waist down," Mr. Casey observed with great emphasis. "In other words, he cannot even save his own life in an emergency. Is it right that we have such a man as President?"

This was the first time I had heard such an argument. I could not answer Mr. Casey's rhetorical question. But what was more important to me was that in the United States, a citizen was free to criticize the head of state.

What a strange country this was!

Chapter

11

College at Last

For the first part of the summer term at "Y" College, I took three courses, namely Economics, English, and Far Eastern History. There was plenty of homework from the start, taking up all of my evenings well into the small hours.

Having quit working at the coffee shop, however, I could not afford to remain unemployed. Again, through the employment service of the college, I found another job prospect. This time, it was as a receptionist at what was described to me as a mental case hospital. As explained to me by the person in charge, the terms were attractive: room, board, and laundry plus thirty dollars a month in cash. And the hospital was a mere twenty-minute streetcar ride from the college. All this for working from 5:00 P.M. to 9:30 P.M. every other day during the week and from 1:00 P.M. to 9:30 P.M. either Saturday or Sunday.

Fairway Sanitarium was located on South Prairie Avenue. When I reported to Mr. Casey about this employment possibility, the lawyer thought it sounded good. He knew the location of the hospital; it had been an exclusive residential area decades before. The hospital for the mentally ill, he presumed, was formerly one of the millionaires' homes.

I realized that Mr. Casey was right as I stood before the door of an imposing mansion on the afternoon of Thursday, July 1, 1943. But there was something depressing about the structure, reminding me of Poe's House of Usher. Its weatherbeaten brick walls were heavily covered with ivy and the spiked iron fence with rust. "I know not how it was—but, with the first glimpse of the building," to quote the writer, "a sense of insufferable gloom pervaded my spirit."

I heard a jingle of many keys and the door opened. I was led in by a fiftyish woman with a gaunt, wrinkled face, on which deep red lipstick seemed incongruous. The inside of the building turned out to be even more depressing than the outside because of a pervading mild stench mixed with odors of medicines common in hospitals.

In the office of this private sanitarium, I was met by a thirtyish woman who said she was secretary to Dr. Perkins, the director. The terms were the same as I had heard from the college employment service. One minor variation was that on the days when I was on duty, I would be on call overnight until the following morning. This meant that when my services were needed, nurses on night duty would request my assistance. But this happened only a few times a month, I was told. It sounded like a perfect arrangement for a self-supporting student. Also, I was curious to see the inner workings of an American mental hospital.

On July 6 I left the YMCA Hotel and moved into Fairway Sanitarium. My work station was a desk just outside the director's office, from which I commanded a good view of the front door and the staircase. I was also able to see a large portion of the living room where many convalescent patients lounged. When a visitor, invariably a relative of a patient, came, I would open the door with a key, register the items brought by the visitor and make sure that these included no knives, matches, or lighters. I discovered that all the doors, even those to the kitchen and bathrooms, were locked. Windows were allowed to be opened only by a person with keys.

The first few days of my life at Fairway were uneventful. I had vaguely anticipated that a mental hospital would be a very noisy place because of the term "bedlam." Yet Fairway, the first mental institution I ever set foot in, was weirdly quiet, even dismal. The patients in the dim living room were usually playing solitaire or mumbling something to themselves.

But I was told not to drop my guard because a seemingly normal patient might suddenly turn violent.

At night, visitors were few, enabling me to study at the desk. At dinner time, I was waited on by Miss Clark, the middleaged woman who had admitted me on my first day. I learned that she was actually a patient, for whom light duties were a therapy. My new job, in fact, seemed like a good deal except for two minor difficulties. First, the shower room in the basement was not an exemplar of cleanliness. Second, I was prematurely awakened at about seven every morning by the jabberings of night-duty nurses preparing their breakfast in the kitchen, which was separated from my room by only a frosted-glass door.

After four days at Fairway, however, my assessment of the new job had to be revised. July 10 was a Saturday, on which I was on duty from 1:00 P.M. to 9:30 P.M. At about eleven, when I had returned to my room after a shower, the bell rang loudly in my room. I put on a bathrobe and dashed upstairs. I left my eyeglasses behind, remembering the instructions that I should not wear them when dealing with a violent patient.

At the entrance to the six-bed ward for men on the third floor, one of the nurses, Miss Johnson, was waiting for me with a syringe in hand.

"Be careful because he is violent," she said without any sign of nervousness, as though she were speaking of a routine matter. I presumed the nurses were used to such situations.

I was told to hold a patient still so that the nurse could administer a sedative by hypodermic injection. Entering the ward, I found a raving patient whose body was shaking while strapped down to the bedframe. With his every motion the whole bed jumped. His five roommates had vacated their own beds and sought refuge in a corner, huddling together terrified. I had been told that one of the main things to remember when dealing with mental patients was to treat them as though they were completely normal no matter what nonsense they might speak.

"Now, let's take it easy," I said, approaching the patient, who was light-complexioned and in his mid-thirties. I placed my hands on his left arm to hold it still. With a mighty jerk, he nearly threw me off balance, making me realize that I was up against a formidable adversary.

"Let's be reasonable," I tried again. I was successful this time in holding down his thick, hairy arm. The nurse nimbly gave him the injection. As I listened to what the patient was saying, I was able to discern some sentences.

"What happened to Henry Ford? . . . What happened to Walter Huston?" These made sense. But "Who blew up Honeymoon Bridge?" stumped me as I wondered about the location of the "bridge," whose name sounded vaguely familiar. It was only on the following day that I realized the name was not one of a bridge but of a card game.

After about five minutes the sedative seemed to take effect. Now much quieter, the patient watched me intently and curiously, as if to figure out who I might be.

Then he began to mumble to himself, to my amusement: "Jay ay pee, jay ay pee . . ." Soon he fell asleep.

Toward the evening of the next day, I went up to the third floor to inquire after the violent patient of the night before. I found him sitting placidly in a chair in the hall, a totally different person. If the nurse hadn't pointed him out, I would not have been able to identify him as the wild man of the preceding night.

"You were pretty violent last night," I said. The patient, whose name was Stanislav Krasinski, welcomed my visiting with him. He was intensely interested in what he had said, of which he himself had no recollection. I repeated what I had heard, and he appeared to find satisfaction in hearing it, as though his utterings had some significance known only to himself.

Stan, as he was called in the sanitarium, said he was a second-generation Pole, his parents having come to America as immigrants. Until a few days before, he had worked at a large transportation company as an office clerk. Because of the heavy workload, he was physically and mentally fatigued. But when he went to see a doctor, he was told: "If you can't do the job, why don't they hire someone else who can?"

"I told the doctor, 'Go to hell!' and left," Stan said. The next day, two policemen came to his place of work and took him to the psychiatry department of the Cook County Hospital. He did not recall anything about what had happened after that. But, he said, the nurses at Fairway found signs of physical abuse on him when he was brought there.

As days passed, his condition improved, and I was pleased to find him being allowed to spend days in the living room. He showed me a mimeographed magazine he had published in May of the same year. It carried poems written by him that cursed war and sang of the ultimate victory of the worker. "They are at the end of the rope; we are at the beginning of hope," one of the stanzas said. He said the writer he respected most was Upton Sinclair.

Learning I was from Japan, Stan said he rated highly Toyohiko Kagawa, a Japanese evangelist then well known among American Christians. He also composed for me an impromptu poem about the Buddha.

Later, I encountered a patient even more powerful than Stan. He was a farmer from a suburb of Chicago. One day, his family noticed he was raising chickens in the basement of his house, and they brought him to Fairway. When I was told by a nurse to restrain this patient, I began with small talk, asking, "What do you raise, Mr. Johnson?"

"I raise hell," he answered quietly.

I ran leather straps around his wrists, which were as thick as beer bottles, and padlocked them to the bedframe as the patient lay tamely on his back.

I wondered why I had to be called to do this task when there was no resistance. Then the patient smiled at me with the confidence of an expert at his old trick.

"Shall I show you something?"

He effortlessly raised his forearms from their horizontal position to the vertical, snapping the straps like paper tape.

The nurse and I duly paled at this show of strength. We hastily doubled the straps to successfully restrain the man this time before injecting him with a sedative.

Things quieted down somewhat in the following weeks. I began to grow accustomed to the Fairway routine, and managed to keep up with my coursework as well. One day in class I met a Nisei named Dick Matsuoka, who told me he had come from a War Relocation Center in a mountain state. He was looking for a job, so I introduced him to Fairway, where he was hired immediately. Dick became my roommate and soon we were close friends.

Working at the reception desk turned out to be the easiest part of the job. Understandably, the patients allowed to stay in the lounge were able to carry on normal conversation. When they would come to me or Dick to ask for a light, we would make small talk. At least one middleaged man talked continuously. This, I was told, was a sign of his mental problem.

One of the women patients, Mrs. Green, was thirtyish and seemingly normal, at least as far as I was able to observe her in the lounge. I wondered why she was hospitalized.

One Sunday afternoon when Dick and I were on duty, the nurses on the second floor called for both of us to come upstairs to the women's ward. Sprinting upstairs along with Dick, I wondered which patient it concerned. I was surprised to find the nurses around Mrs. Green's bed, trying to administer a sedative. I was further surprised to see her lying on her back in bed, revealing her voluptuous, if slightly dark, body without a stitch on.

Dick was about my height—five feet four—chubby and very light complexioned with clean-cut features. The two of us cautiously approached the bed, no doubt wearing similar looks of apprehension. Embarrassed as I was to find Mrs. Green in this state of undress, I expected her to treat me like an old friend because we had chatted normally many times before. But obviously she was a different person now, and this was the very reason we had been summoned.

Viewing Dick and me—standing side by side at the foot of her bed—like strangers, Mrs. Green observed with a smirk: "What's this? Japanese Army trying to rape me?"

What a sense of humor! It was perfect. Two ethnic Japanese, including an enemy alien to boot, called in to help nurses give a hypo to an utterly defenseless American woman!

We burst out laughing. But the nurses seemed embarrassed, probably because they thought Matsuoka and I felt insulted. One of them blushed and chided Mrs. Green, "What nonsense you talk!"

Having made her quip, the patient seemed totally satisfied that she was in complete control of the situation. Nonetheless, our presence evidently proved effective. Mrs. Green agreed not only to cover her body but also to surrender herself to an injection without our having to lay a finger on her.

When the first half of the summer term at the Central YMCA College ended on August 20, 1943, I had earned nine credit hours—my first in an American college. Three days later, the second part of the term began. This time I registered for Psychology, Geology, and English. These classes lasted until September 10, offering the equivalent of a semester's work in less than four weeks. It meant highly concentrated class work—as much as three hours of each course in a single day.

I struggled while working at Fairway. Since I was still interested in matriculating at the University of Chicago, however, I called on its director of admissions on September 13 to inquire about the autumn term. I was told that Japanese students from the West Coast could not be accepted.

"Why?" I asked of the director, Miss Wickam. She said this was by Army order: A secret experiment was going on at the university, as was the case at Northwestern as well.

Little did I suspect then that what she referred to was the super-sensitive plan to produce an atomic bomb, codenamed the Manhattan Project.

As at Northwestern, the director of admissions at Chicago said I would be informed as soon as the ban was lifted. Until such time, she said encouragingly, I should continue to earn credits at the Central YMCA College.

Back at the college on the following day, I registered for English, Political Science, German, Economics, and Biology, paying a tuition fee of 120 dollars. The autumn term, which opened on September 20, was to end on January 28, 1944.

Toward the end of this term, I received what I thought was good news from the Student Relocation Committee at Philadelphia, a civic organization run by the Society of Friends to help Nisei enter college from War Relocation Centers. Though I was not a Nisei, I had availed myself of the service of this committee. The news was that the University of Chicago was now admitting "Japanese students" and, therefore, I should contact Miss Wickam.

I immediately called on the director of admissions again. She said there was now some possibility for entrance, and in preparation I should take an aptitude test, which was required of all applicants.

I took the test on the morning of Saturday, January 29. I thought I did fairly well, but it was somewhat demoralizing to see that my fellow examinees were all young boys and girls of about fifteen. The University of Chicago, then under the tutelage of Chancellor Robert Maynard Hutchins, had the unique system of awarding the degree of Bachelor of Arts to students who were admitted after completing not twelve, but ten years of primary and secondary education. This degree, which came to be known as the "Chicago B.A.," however, was not considered by other educational institutions as being on a par with the conventional Bachelor of Arts degree.

On the following Monday, January 31, I spent all day at the university, taking the placement test. When I returned to Fairway Sanitarium that evening, another letter from the Student Relocation Council was awaiting me. It said that the University of Chicago was still not admitting alien Japanese students. Apparently, the "good news" I had received was premature due to confusion about the meaning of "Japanese students," which had been used to refer to Japanese-Americans. An enemy alien like me, I was told, had to obtain approval from the Provost Marshal's Office. The letter enclosed an application form, which I instantly filled out and mailed.

On the following day, I was back again at Miss Wickam's office to hear the results of the tests I had taken. I was pleasantly surprised that they were quite satisfactory and, particularly, that I was "above average" in English composition. This, I thought, was a high reward for my struggles to learn English during the two years since I arrived in the United States.

In the spring term of "Y" College that began on February 7, I signed up for five courses: English Literature, German, Sociology, Natural Sciences, and American History. Still, I was anxious to experience a campus life as such, and my choice was still the University of Chicago. I had seen its Gothic architecture and green lawns and heard of its academic reputation. To maximize my chances of obtaining permission to study at the university, on March 3, 1944, I penned a letter to the PMO, asking them to expedite the processing of my application.

A response came on April 14—but not in the form of special permission. Things were not that easy, to be sure. The PMO's reply to my letter was a visit to the college by an investigator.

Hardly a military type but more of an intellectual, the official, in mufti, made every effort to learn about me. His questions delved into the smallest corners of my life back in Japan, particularly the education I had received. Likewise with the members of my family—how old they were and what they did.

He was particularly interested in my views on the state, Shinto, Buddhism, and the Emperor. His primary interest was in whether or not I was a spy or a saboteur who would sacrifice his life for the state.

It would have been far simpler if only he had asked me that question straight out. But obviously he would not accept a negative

answer, which he anticipated. He kept asking maddeningly periph-
eral questions, so he could surmise my real answer on the basis of my
responses.

"Do you believe in the hereafter?" he asked, using a word I did
not know.

"What do you mean by 'hereafter'?"

"Life after death."

"Then, no," I said.

He did, he said, perhaps to induce me to agree with him and then
trip me up. He was a Catholic, he revealed, and because he believed
in life after death, his having lost his father early on did not sadden
him at all. This I found difficult to believe.

Yet the persistence of this interrogation was beginning to intrigue
me, if not wear me out. This, too, seemed to be a purposely
employed technique. I began to feel I was playing a game of wits
against a man at least ten years older than I. If I could beat him, I
thought I could be proud of myself.

I countered by asking *him* questions to provoke him. But he was
no mean adversary. In the end, I felt dizzy, with a headache and
flushed face. Altogether the interview lasted three and a half hours.
The investigator said nothing about his evaluation of me before he
left. Confident he had found nothing dangerous about me, I waited
for a letter offering me special status, but none came.

The Army ban against Japanese students from the West Coast
was not the only reminder of the war being waged between Japan
and the United States. The streets of Chicago were festooned with
posters carrying slogans such as "Beat the Japs" and a slant-eyed,
high-cheekboned, and buck-toothed Oriental face. The United States
mail truck carried the warning, "Loose Talk Does Reach Tokyo—
Let's Stop It!" under such a caricature.

My summary impression of the American image of the Japanese
since Pearl Harbor was one to which all pejorative adjectives, beginning with "treacherous" and including "sadistic," "barbaric," "bestial," "insidious," "pernicious," "diabolical," "demonic," and on and

on, were applied. Yet this did not distress me at all, because I knew these adjectives did not apply to me. I was none of these.

If anything, I wanted to demonstrate the falsity of such an image through my own conduct and by simply being in the midst of an America at war. In this respect, I could not have better timed—though of course unwittingly—my arrival in Chicago in late May 1943. As though having waited for me to come out of a War Relocation Center, within a few days of my arrival in Chicago the United States government launched the Third War Bond Drive by stirring up hatred for Japan and patriotism for America. For such a purpose the government detonated the best possible ammunition—the story of the Bataan Death March, which occurred sometime around April 1942, in the Philippines.

Despite all this, nowhere did I encounter open hostility on a personal basis. Mr. Casey, my mentor in Chicago, had told me that Chicagoans were "too busy to stop to wonder" about whether an Oriental-looking person in the street was Japanese, Chinese, Filipino, or American Indian. This I found to be true.

A rare exception occurred one cold morning in early 1944. I was to take a streetcar for downtown from a stop near Fairway Sanitarium. As I arrived at the safety island, a fellow commuter, a middleaged American, smiled at me and said, "Good morning! Some good news from the front, eh?"

A friendly fellow, I thought. But then I was puzzled because I could not think of any recent instance of the Japanese winning a battle. A moment later, I realized that this stranger was congratulating me on an engagement won by Nationalist Chinese forces somewhere in China.

His mistaken assumption about my national background was amusing, bringing a smile to my face, which again he must have misconstrued. Not anxious to spoil his misplaced goodwill, I did not take the trouble to correct his false assumption.

A more tangible reminder of the war was an exhibit held at Marshall Field's department store of souvenirs brought back from

Attu by a newspaper correspondent. The small island in the Aleutians was seized by Japanese forces on October 30, 1942, but the 2,500 troops were annihilated on May 29, 1943, by attacking American forces.

The items on display which I viewed, unable to breathe, included a rifle, bayonet, helmet, canteen, and a torn Rising Sun flag. But there were items that evidently defied the imagination of Americans. One of them, labeled "incense bag," was actually a powder puff, a rust-proofing device for military swords. A paper balloon, which I presumed had been contained in one of the packages sent to the fighting men on the front to boost their morale, was captioned as a "lantern."

A worse disaster for Japan than the loss of Attu was the battle of Tarawa and Makin in the Gilbert Islands in the South Pacific. While working at the mental hospital, I pored over newspaper reports on the attack, which lasted for seventy-six hours from the afternoon of November 20, 1943, in one of the bloodiest campaigns of World War II. The press coverage ended with front-page pictures of Japanese marines who had killed themselves by pulling the triggers of their own rifles rather than surrender. In Japan, the loss of Tarawa and Makin was publicized as a glorious illustration of the fighting spirit of the Japanese. Rear Admiral Keiji Shibasaki, commander of the garrison, who perished with his 5,400 men, was extolled as a veritable war hero. Only later did I find that by a strange coincidence Shibasaki was an alumnus of my Ono Middle School, the only admiral at that.

While I was at Poston, I had read in the November 30, 1942, issue of *Time* magazine about fighting in New Guinea, in which Lt. Gen. Tomitaro Horii was described as being in a tough spot with his battered troops. In trying to recoup, he had lost a cruiser and two destroyers, "blown to pieces by U.S. and Australian pilots." I learned after the end of the war that by the time the news magazine printed his name, the general was dead. But the magazine report left an indelible mark on my mind because General Horii's name was well known to me. He was the only general among the alumni of Ono Middle School.

This meant, though I did not know it at the time, that my alma mater lost the only general and admiral among its alumni in two of the toughest battles of the Pacific War—both in November one year apart.

On July 15, 1943, I had received a letter from the Department of State in Washington, D.C., enclosing an application form for repatriation to Japan on a second exchange ship, which was to be the last throughout the war years. Firmly committed to the pursuit of my objective, I did not consider repatriation; to go home at that point would have been an ignominious defeat in my private war. Yet this invitation to return home unavoidably aroused nostalgia in me, keeping me awake until one o'clock the following morning.

I wanted to learn why the State Department had sent me such a letter. Was it because the Japanese government had requested my repatriation? Or had my father asked the government to put me on the list of repatriates?

If the request for repatriation had come from the Japanese government, refusal would constitute treason. I would have no choice but to board the ship despite my firm resolve to finish my coursework. And my two years of struggle in America would end without the reward of a college degree.

On the afternoon of July 16, I went to the office of the Red Cross Society in Chicago to send a cable to my father, saying:

> I am fine. Studying here. Did you request repatriation?
> Please reply. Kiyoaki.

The cable was sent out on July 29, I was informed later. While I wondered when I might receive the reply and what its contents would be, a Red Cross message from my parents was forwarded to me from Poston. This was not a reply to my July cable. Dated January 7, 1943, the typed Japanese missive said:

> Don't lose heart, Kiyoaki. Be in high spirits even if you
> cannot study. We will ask for your repatriation by next
> ship. Father and Mother.

I was pleased to learn that it had been my parents, not the government of Japan, that wanted me to come home. Their action was totally understandable. With my first Red Cross message of the autumn of 1942, which I sent from Poston, they learned I was in a "detention camp," as the War Relocation Center was described in Japan. This must have made me seem like a POW, hardly in a position to pursue my goal of studying in school. They assumed that I would be kept there for the duration of the war—a tragic waste of time—even though I said I would not come home until I accomplished my objective.

In my initial communication, I had told my parents to "trust your son." But they could not see how I could be trusted as far as the pursuit of my goal was concerned. The best thing they could think of doing for me was to seek my repatriation.

So my father had applied to the Japanese Foreign Ministry for my repatriation as early as October 1942. Despite the State Department's notice, my resolve remained unaltered. Accordingly, the State Department transmitted my negative response to the government of Japan. The Foreign Ministry official in charge of Japanese subjects in enemy countries wrote a letter, dated August 11, 1943, to my father. It informed him that the United States government ascertained the will of each of the Japanese whose repatriation was sought.

"We have received a cable," he wrote, "saying that your son Kiyoaki refused to return." The official offered a possible explanation for this surprising response from me: "Being in an enemy country, your son probably failed to grasp our intent or possibly misconstrued the repatriation offer by the Department of State as a ruse despite the fact that the U.S. government was acting only according to our request.

"We did reply, however," the letter went on, "that it was his father who was requesting repatriation. In any event, your son himself does not appear anxious to return home. Even if he does not, you need not worry; there are still many Japanese students in the United States."

The tone of the letter was one that was intended to comfort my parents for failing to have their son come home.

Meanwhile, the Japanese Red Cross Society, too, passed on my cable of inquiry. It was transmitted to my father by a letter of August 11 from the POW Relief Committee of the society.

Later, when the Japanese Foreign Ministry received the list of repatriates on the exchange ship, the office concerned again wrote to my father on September 20 to inform him that my name was not on it.

Despite this note, my father did send me a reply cable through the Red Cross, which I received in Chicago on October 9. It said in English: "Arranged authorities for repatriation. Return. Father Murata Itsuji."

Assuming that he would learn my negative response, I wanted to make certain he understood the reason for that. On January 22, 1944, I sent another message through the Red Cross:

> Dear Father: I am in excellent health. Studying hard in college. People are cordial. Have no worries. Regards to all. Kiyoaki Murata.

When they read this note on April 22, 1944, my parents were indeed elated. Their son was now in an American college, studying! The Japanese translation of "people are cordial" as translated into Japanese by the Red Cross, was "*minna shinsetsudesu*," which meant "all [Americans] are kind."

My parents, however, did not know if this part was true. Their uncertainty was partly due to a comment made by one of my middle school classmates, Itaro Kondo. Itaro had become an officer in the tank regiment at Aonogahara near Kawai Mura, and he would occasionally visit with my parents to inquire about me. When he saw my message, he told my parents that I had been forced by Americans to write they were all kind.

This reaction in post–Pearl Harbor Japan was not unreasonable. People of the United States and Britain were described in wartime propaganda as "fiends and animals." Such people could not possibly be kind to Japanese in the United States. Folks at home could not imagine me working my way through college without being harassed by these barbarians.

Another Japanese-American, also a student at the Central YMCA College, worked at the sanitarium with me. His name was Jeff Sawada, and I did not know much about his background except for the fact that he had been born in Hawaii. He had a room to himself on the second floor of a separate building in the backyard. The building still housed a dust-covered coach, a legacy from the meat-packer millionaire of yesteryear the mansion had belonged to. The second floor contained several rooms that once must have served as quarters for servants.

One day, Jeff dropped into my room—an unusual event.

"I went to the police department today to ask for a license to carry a gun," Jeff announced without preface.

Amazed, I asked why.

"To protect myself."

Even more amazed, I queried, "To protect yourself from whom?"

"*Hakujin*," was Jeff's reply.

"How ridiculous," I said, half laughing. "Jeff, look at me. I am an enemy alien—straight from Japan. But I have never felt the need for a weapon to protect myself against Americans around me. You are an American citizen. This is your own country. Why should you think of such a thing?"

"I don't trust them," he muttered.

"But did the police give you a license?"

"No, they didn't."

"They shouldn't, either. If a fellow like you carried a gun around, it would be dangerous."

"I feel sorry for *hakujin*," Jeff said weakly and left without describing whatever experience he might have had that prompted him to attempt obtaining a license to carry a firearm.

January 1, 1944, was the third New Year's I celebrated in America. But it was hardly a holiday for me because several of the nurses took the day off, which meant I had to work continuously from nine in the morning till nine at night. A special chore that fell to me on this day was feeding the patients on the second and third floors by carrying trays to and from the dumbwaiter.

I was beginning to weary of my routine of working at the sanitarium. My diary during the first part of January of this year is marked by such entries as "I feel tired," "Tired," "Poor appetite," "Worked all day long," and so on, indicating my discontented state.

Furthermore, I began to feel that the gloomy, unhealthy atmosphere of the hospital was having an effect on my own mind. Concerned about my mental welfare, I decided to leave the sanitarium.

Looking for an apartment proved futile. Signs of "Room for rent" were abundant, but whenever I rang a doorbell, the owner would say, "It's just been taken." At one place, the landlady was honest. She said, "I rent my rooms only to gentiles." Her use of the word "gentile" amused me.

The experience reminded me of that of Wang Yuan, the hero of Pearl Buck's *A House Divided*. It gave me a strange sense of being a protagonist in a novel.

In the end, I was able to rent an apartment in a large three-story wooden house on Sixty-first Street, not far from the University of Chicago. On May 6, 1944, I moved into the new abode after ten months of life and work at Fairway Sanitarium.

Chapter
12

My Longest Day

The spring term at Central Y ended in mid-June. Having been liberated from the depressing milieu of the mental hospital, I was enjoying a rare sense of relaxation in my apartment on June 19, 1944. It was a cool, pleasant Monday.

At about 10:00 A.M., the front buzzer rang. I answered and found a large, stocky man in the hallway.

"Is Mrs. Rasmussen home?" the visitor asked. Mrs. Rasmussen, to my knowledge, was the proprietress of this apartment house but I had never met her. Probably a widow, she was living in California comfortably, I presumed, with income from her asset in Chicago.

"No, she lives in California," I informed the stranger.

The man produced what appeared to be an identification card from an inside pocket of his jacket.

"Are you Murata? My name is Orton. I am from the FBI."

"Yes, I am Murata."

"I want to ask you a few questions."

"O.K. Please come in," I said, opening the door to my one-room apartment, which contained a large desk—a former family dining table—and a double bed.

My heart began pounding, but I told myself not to betray my feelings. I waved the FBI man to one of the old sofas in the furnished apartment, and he sat down.

"You must be busy nowadays," I said, primarily to be sociable while thinking of what I had read about the FBI and its wartime responsibilities. Tension was building up within me. Why did this G-man come to see me at this time? I could not think of any particular reason for any sudden interest the federal agency might have in me. If there was any need to question me, the FBI could have done so much earlier.

"Could you come to our downtown office?"

"Sure," I said, looking for a memo pad. "We are on vacation now. What's your address?"

"I have a car outside. I want you to come with me."

Right now? The scene was beginning to look like a movie, but it was no fun. My mind flashed back to the FBI's visit to Mr. Shimizu's house back in San Leandro. Was I to be carted off for several days of questioning? I put on a suit and sat in the passenger seat of Mr. Orton's not-too-deluxe sedan. From Sixty-first Street, the agent swung his car over to Lake Shore Drive. Dark and depressing thoughts filled my head, making the sun seem incongruously bright on the greenery along the way. What was he up to? Why did he want to question me in his office?

"Where is your home?" Mr. Orton inquired, eyes on the road.

"Hyogo Prefecture." Knowing that this made little sense to him, I added, "Kobe is the prefectural capital."

"Kobe must have been pretty badly damaged by now," Mr. Orton said half to himself.

"Really? Do you know a lot about Kobe?" I asked, thinking that the FBI might have more information than what I could read in the newspapers, all the while visualizing the port city as it looked in June 1941.

"You shouldn't be asking *me* questions," said the agent.

The Chicago office of the Federal Bureau of Investigation was on the sixteenth floor of the Bankers Building on South Dearborn Street. The room I was led into was small, with two desks and three chairs. I noted that the window was covered with heavy wire mesh, which I presumed was for preventing anyone from leaping out—for whatever reason.

There was another agent there, a lean man, who sat a few feet away from me and Mr. Orton, probably indicating his junior position.

The interrogation began with routine information—my name, address, age, and then, inevitably, why I had come to America.

To the last question, I said that I wanted to study in America to learn about American democracy. This, of course, was partially true. But I avoided giving the more important reason—my wanting to subject myself to the hardships of working one's way through school in a foreign land. I knew from my experience with other Americans that this motivation of mine might not be readily understood and accepted by my questioners.

Apparently my answer did not satisfy the agents. Why should the government of Japan allow me to get out of the country only six months before the outbreak of the war when I was eighteen years old? It seemed that at that time all Americans assumed that the Japanese government had a definite plan to attack the United States as early as June 1941, though the fact is that it did not.

I was under military age, which was twenty in Japan, I explained. I received a passport from the Japanese government because I met all the conditions needed, likewise with the American consulate general in Kobe that issued me a visa.

The agents wanted to know what subjects we studied in middle school in Japan. I enumerated all, including military training and martial arts, for which there was a choice of two. I told them I had taken kendo, not judo.

"For military training, what kind of weapon did you use?"

"The regulation Army rifle."

"Machine guns?"

"Yes, machine guns, too."

"Did you have field exercises? How often?"

"Once every school term in our fifth year."

Suddenly, the other man opened up.

"By the way, I understand you're quite a crack shot."

The remark stunned me. How could he have known that I participated in the national athletic meet in Tokyo in the rifle shooting division in 1940? I had admired the FBI for its efficiency in the past. Yet even they could not possibly have begun investigating me before I left Japan. The answer, however, came to me some time later when I regained presence of mind. I must have somehow mentioned this shooting match to the investigator from the Provost Marshal's Office a few months earlier. This seemed to prove there was at least some liaison between the U.S. Army and the FBI.

"No, I am not a crack shot. If you mean my taking part in the national shooting event, it was only by a fluke."

The reason for the FBI's interest in this particular element in my background occurred to me two decades later—in the early 1960s. If I had been sent to the United States with a mission to kill an important individual, marksmanship would have been an important qualification indeed.

"Do you think the Emperor is a god?"

"Heavens no," I stressed. "No educated Japanese thinks so."

I gave my explanations of Shinto and Buddhism. Shinto was a form of nature worship, animism, that attributes spirits to natural objects and animals. An outstanding human being after death was often considered a supernatural entity—*kami* (deity). Unfortunately, I said, the same Japanese word was applied to the Christian God. I told them this was the reason Americans were upset by Japanese reverence toward the Emperor, who was often described as a "living god."

I went on to say that Buddhism, on the other hand, was a dead religion because it had become totally institutionalized. Japanese went to Buddhist temples only a few times a year and Buddhist priests came to their parishioners' homes only to officiate at funeral and memorial services.

Changing the subject, Mr. Orton asked, "Do you have a Rising Sun flag?"

"Now," I said to myself, "don't tell me you were watching me as I left Kobe, waving a small flag to my well-wishers on the pier. I know your system is good, but it couldn't be that good." The fact was I did have two Rising Sun flags when I left Japan. But both were destroyed by Aunt Kané in San Leandro after Pearl Harbor. Mr. Orton's question was posed in the present tense—"Do you have. . . ?"—not in the past tense.

"No," I replied.

The agent did not pursue the subject. A few hours later, I realized the reason why he did not: He knew he could find out if I was lying.

As time elapsed with a succession of questions and answers, my throat began to hurt and my face became flushed, just as when I had my bout with the Provost Marshal's Office interrogator.

Considerable tensions were building up in me, in fact. I had nothing to hide, to begin with. Therefore, all I had to do was to give a straight answer to each question. But what if they didn't believe me? One suspicious reply and they could send me directly to a camp for dangerous aliens, and I might never achieve my goal.

I had an obligation to return to Japan as soon as possible, because I had had my military service deferred. If I were to be placed in a detention center now, all I had done so far would come to naught.

In January of that year, I had met a Japanese-American lawyer named Min Yasui in town. He seemed amazed that a Japanese student like me was able to go to school at all in Chicago. "You are very lucky," he had said. "I know there are fifty-four Japanese students at the detention center for enemy aliens in Santa Fe, New Mexico."

I had thought at the time that I was indeed lucky. Now, I told myself, somehow I must survive this questioning session without ending up in Santa Fe—or wherever. To ensure my continued struggle toward my goal, I had to give answers that would satisfy my interrogators.

At the same time, I became overcome with a sense of heroism about what I was doing: engaging two G-Men, who were physically far bigger and older by at least a dozen years than I, in what I regarded as an intense verbal battle. And in this engagement, my supreme mission was at stake. So far, I thought, I was doing pretty well without telling any lies or otherwise compromising my personal ethics.

Mr. Orton, meanwhile, appeared to think he was not getting the kind of response from me that he wanted, that is, one for which he could send me—assuming that is what he wanted—to a detention center.

The federal agent decided to try a new tack—a rather imaginative one at that.

"You have a brother," he said.

"Yes. I told you. He is fifteen years younger than I. So, he is now seven years old."

"Suppose your brother joined the Japanese Army and was sent to the United States as a spy or a saboteur and he came to your apartment asking you to shelter him—what would you do?"

I swallowed hard. I knew this was an important question, a big trap, that might doom my immediate future. It was obvious that the answer he hoped to elicit from me would be: "Of course, I will protect him—to help him perform his mission." If I said that, Mr. Orton could decide unequivocally that I qualified as a dangerous enemy alien. That would abort my blossoming educational career in the United States. But how could I get around this obvious snare without involving my conscience? This question, indeed, called for judicious handling.

"My younger brother is only seven years old," I repeated slowly, looking at both agents. They nodded.

"You say if he joined the Japanese Army. This is sheer hypothesis, isn't it? He is a child. So your question is a totally hypothetical one. Right?"

"Yeah," Mr. Orton said with a barely perceptible nod.

The premise that this was a "totally hypothetical question" was of crucial importance to me. I pictured my brother, Kazushige, as the happy and lively elf I was reluctant to leave behind in 1941.

Now I was being compelled to visualize him as a "Japanese soldier." Conjuring up an image of a soldier in a khaki uniform, complete with puttees over the boots, was easy enough. But the idea of such a figure coming to me at 1516 East Sixty-first Street, Chicago, Illinois, to seek asylum seemed ludicrous. What's more, I could not put any face over the uniform for the simple reason that I had never tried to envision Kazushige at age twenty.

As far as I was concerned, there would indeed be no such individual; no such possibility. That thought freed me from any moral obligation to be truthful about what I might or might not do. The question was simply irrelevant because I could not foresee the preposterous situation.

"So," I said, "I can give you only a hypothetical answer." With this premise, I could not hold myself responsible for whatever I might say. My hypothetical answer to a hypothetical question, as far as I was concerned, had no consequence at all.

"I will help him surrender himself to the authorities," I said. "There is no point in his monkeying around here."

Surprisingly, the agents did not pursue the subject further. I thought I had won this round. Now perhaps I could be released to go home.

I was wrong. Mr. Orton had something else up his sleeve.

"Since you arrived in Chicago last year, have you visited any other town?"

"Well, I went to Evanston."

"What for?"

"To inquire about enrolling in Northwestern University."

"Did you get a travel permit before going there?"

"Travel permit?" It had never occurred to me that Evanston was outside the jurisdiction of the U.S. District Attorney in Chicago, because one could go to Evanston by getting on a train on the Loop Line and riding for only an hour. "No, I didn't," I said.

"In that case," observed Mr. Orton, "you violated a federal regulation. I'm afraid I'll have to send you to the D.A.'s Office."

It was past one o'clock in the afternoon.

"When you are through with the D.A., you may have lunch and then come back here," said Mr. Orton.

The D.A.'s Office was on the second floor of the Federal Building, across the street from the Bankers.

When I arrived at the receptionist's window on the second floor of the large black edifice with a big courtyard for parking, an attractive female secretary said, "Mr. Murata?"

This I found genuinely flattering. Like a VIP I was closely watched, my every step traced. I was directed to go into one of the several rooms whose doors had the label: "Assistant U.S. District Attorney."

The man, who had been expecting me, got up and walked toward me from behind his desk. He was a giant—the largest man I had ever met in America, or anywhere, weighing probably three hundred pounds, more than twice what I did.

"What did you do, what did you do?" the official bellowed. "Please sit down," he said, motioning me to a couch.

"Well," I began. "I have been told by the FBI that I violated a federal regulation without knowing it."

"Oh, never mind federal regulations," roared the giant, to my surprise. His voice was as loud as one might expect from his large bulk. But there was no hint of hostility. In fact, he appeared to be somewhat amused by the situation he had not anticipated until a few minutes before, when he received a telephone call from across the street. Even I sensed something comic in the vast disparity in physical size between the assistant D.A. and myself.

"Let's talk about the war," he said. "Which side do you think will win?"

"Militarily," I said, "the Allies will."

My answer was based on what I had been aware of, reading news of the war. Japan was losing one battle after another—East New Guinea, Guadalcanal, Attu, Tarawa, and other areas in the Pacific.

My questioner could have made an issue of what I meant by qualifying my answer with "militarily." "Could Japan win in any other way?" he could have said. But he did not. Next, he put a rather basic question.

"What are you doing here?"

I said I was going to school, as I should be, since I had come to the United States as a student, describing what I had done since June 1941.

"You are extremely fortunate," the official said. "On December 7, immediately after the war began, every American and Briton in Japan was picked up by the police and put in jail."

"That's not true," I protested. "Not everyone. I have met at least one American missionary who came back here recently by exchange ship. He said he was left in freedom in Japan even after Pearl Harbor—until repatriation."

I was thinking of Dr. Roy Smith, a missionary teacher who had taught in a number of universities in Kobe and Osaka. As one of the repatriates from Japan in 1942, he visited Poston one day and gave a report to the residents about his experiences in post–Pearl Harbor Japan.

The assistant D.A. did not argue with me, obviously because he knew I had firmer ground to stand on than he did regarding this particular subject.

Switching to another, he said, "Do you know that just before the war broke out, the Japanese government sent to the United States thousands of young Japanese whom they had trained in spy schools to act as fifth columnists here after war began?"

"Do you mean to say," I countered vigorously, "you believe the nonsense you read in those yellow papers?"

I was referring to such articles as I myself had read about spies and saboteurs, supposedly trained by the Japanese military and sent into the United States by the thousands before the war. I was not certain if the official was implying that I was one of them.

Again, he did not pursue the subject. He said, "What do you intend to do after the war is over?"

I had no idea of when the war would be over, though I felt it would not last very much longer. But the question was irrelevant to me because the war really had no bearing on my personal plans. I was going to complete a college education program in America and then go home.

Therefore, I said, "I want to stay here until I finish my schooling. I am allowed to do so as long as I am in an authorized school," I said, remembering the premise on which I had been admitted to the United States.

Before I completed the statement, however, I sensed that something had gone wrong.

Sure enough, the official scowled and said, "You talk as though you had the right to stay here and go to school. But I could put you in jail tomorrow if I wanted to."

I knew he was right. He could probably put me in jail right then, as a matter of fact, because I had violated a federal regulation. In fact, this was the office where I should have come to obtain the travel permit.

This was true. Yet the fact remained that if this large official should decide to go through with what he had just threatened, it would wreck my plans. This, I felt, I must avoid at all costs, and fast.

"You know," I began, and paused a moment for a breath. "If you treat me harshly now and put me in jail without allowing me to go to school, I would be going back to Japan with ill feelings about America. On the other hand, if you treat me decently and let me study, how can I, when I go back to Japan, say bad things about this country?"

"That's true," said the official, thoughtfully. From then on our chat concerned trivial things. It seemed like a conversation between old friends. Then the assistant D.A. produced a business card and scribbled a few words on it, telling me to hand it to Mr. Orton. He said he would take no action against me. It seemed that I had won one battle in the war with the FBI.

"Be more careful now," he said with a smile, offering his huge hand as I bade him farewell.

After washing down a hamburger with Coca-Cola, I returned to Mr. Orton's office and presented the card to him. Mr. Orton appeared puzzled by the "no action" note from the assistant D.A.

At last I would be released. I fully expected a "Now you may go" from the agent. It was already about 2:30 P.M.

Instead, Mr. Orton said, "Would you mind if we searched your premises?"

"Not at all," I replied, pretending to be unperturbed despite my disappointment. I signed at the bottom of a form that stated that I had no objection to the agents searching my apartment. I learned years later that the consent form was necessary because there was no specific charge against me.

This time the other agent, Mr. McInerny, as well as Mr. Orton, came to 1516 East Sixty-first Street. In my apartment Mr. Orton worked through my large desk—items on top and in the drawers, mainly letters, diaries, and photographs in my album. Mr. McInerny checked my dresser and its contents. The search was thorough.

"Why do you open letters by neatly cutting an edge?" Mr. Orton asked, examining the letters I had saved.

"Because it's neater that way," I said. But I knew why Agent Orton had asked the question. I had read somewhere that a foreign spy in the United States received secret messages written on a thin strip of paper which was then rolled and installed on the edge of an ordinary-looking envelope.

The federal agent tried to read the impressions on the sheets of carbon paper I had saved by holding them against the light. He examined the pictures in my album, particularly those showing me in middle school life in Japan. Of especial interest to Mr. Orton was one taken in front of Sumiyoshi Shrine, located near our school, on February 11, 1941, when our school held a martial arts tournament. The event was designed to celebrate National Founding Day, a day which, according to the official history, marked the beginning of Japan in 660 B.C. The photograph showed the members of the winning kendo team, including me, with two Rising Sun flags adorning the front of the sanctuary in the background. After the two terms in the rifle club, I had returned to the kendo club with my doctor's permission.

Another item that obviously seized Mr. Orton's attention was the

English translation of *Senjinkun*, the code of conduct for Japanese soldiers my friend Kinsuke Nishimura had sent me in 1941.

At long last the agents were ready to go. I saw to my dismay that they were taking some of my diaries, some letters, the *Senjinkun* translation, and some photos. Mr. Orton assured me that the items would be returned to me when the Bureau was through examining them. But the mere fact that the agents took these items suggested something ominous. Perhaps they were to be used as evidence that I was "dangerous" to the American government after all. I became tense as once again I contemplated the possibility of incarceration. All the efforts I had made toward my goal would come to naught.

That evening I was too exhausted to eat supper, and went to bed at about seven o'clock. For weeks after this long June day, I did not write anything in my diary because I was not certain about how the FBI would react to the contents of the one they had taken away from me. Until I knew the answer, I was reluctant to put down my private thoughts in writing.

Months later I saw Mr. Orton again. On September 7, 1944, I got off an elevator on the sixteenth floor of the Bankers Building and almost walked into none other than Mr. Orton, who was speaking to someone in the hall.

"Hello," I said, smiling. But the special agent looked uncertain, apparently not recognizing me.

"It's me—Murata. You grilled me in June."

This helped, but probably embarrassed him.

"Oh, yes. But you look different today."

I realized that I should not have expected him to recognize me instantly; after all, I was probably one of hundreds he questioned in the course of duty, whereas to me he was simply unforgettable.

I told Mr. Orton that I was leaving town and said, "I wanted to tell you my change of address in advance. Otherwise I might get into trouble again."

My mild sarcasm, however, did not evoke the response I had expected.

"That's fine," said Mr. Orton, beaming and—unlike the previous time—in good humor.

"By the way," I said, taking up another important matter for which I had come to the Bankers Building, "when are you going to return my diaries, et cetera?"

"Oh, we'll return them to you as soon as we are through with them."

It meant that the FBI was still working on them to determine what action they should take with regard to me. But the diaries were returned, as Mr. Orton promised, three months later.

There is another footnote to this story. Thirty-five years later, on June 7, 1979, I held a heavy envelope before me. My heart thumped as I lifted the scissors, as though I were about to read a letter from someone I had loved decades ago.

The sender of the envelope was the Federal Bureau of Investigation in Washington, D.C.

More than half a year before that day, I had been in New York as a delegate from Japan to the thirty-third General Assembly of the United Nations. I had a reunion with an old friend and during our conversation I described my encounter with the FBI. I told my friend I had always been intensely curious about what kind of report Mr. Orton had written about me.

Then my friend said there was a way to find out, referring to the Freedom of Information Act. I had heard about it in Japan.

"But that applies only to American citizens, doesn't it?" I said.

"Well, you can try to find out," said my friend.

I made a telephone call to the New York office of the FBI and was given an address to write to. Correspondence followed between Washington and me during the first part of 1979. And then finally the file arrived—the FBI file which, if it had not been for the Freedom of Information Act, I would never have been allowed to see.

The four-paged, single-spaced typewritten report headlined "Chicago File 100–15940" began with minor facts about myself and my movements, addresses where I stayed in the United States, with several surprising but unimportant inaccuracies.

I flipped through one page after another, looking for a reference to the bout of wits Mr. Orton and I had had concerning my brother's hypothetical arrival in Chicago as a Japanese military agent. For thirty-five years I had thought of this as the high point of the half-day war of words. But what I found in the file was sorely disappointing.

> Subject was asked what he would do in the event that a Japanese saboteur or Japanese spy called on him and sought aid and asked for room and board.

So this was how Mr. Orton summed up the exchange of words on that issue. No reference to the idea that it would be my brother; no reference to my point that we were speaking hypothetically. And my reply, according to Mr. Orton, was simply this:

> The subject immediately replied that he would immediately turn them over to the American authorities.

Some of the topics dealt with in the report had completely slipped my mind during the decades after 1944. These included Japan's foreign policy toward the rest of Asia, the State Department offer of repatriation for me, my inquiry about how it came about, and so forth.

One passage flabbergasted me:

> The subject admitted that he was an *opportunist* [author's italics] and considered himself well off because inasmuch as he was in the United States he did not have to fight because he was an alien, and he was finding himself in a rather good position during the war.

I could not have possibly said I was an "opportunist" because I had always regarded such a person with supreme disdain. Even in the context of the interrogation, this was impossible. Most probably, this was a case of either a stenographic error or Mr. Orton's mishearing me because of my inarticulate pronunciation. In reply to a question or a prompting, I probably said I considered myself "fortunate" because I did not fight in war as a soldier while being able to continue my studies in the United States.

The agent also reported that I said I was an atheist. "However," he went on, "it should be noted that several of the documents which have been forwarded to the Bureau for translation contained religious references." As far as I can ascertain, the only item seized that had any religious significance was the photograph taken in front of the shrine.

Concerning the search of my apartment, for which I "executed a waiver," the report said, "no contraband was found . . . but a number of diaries and documents and letters were found which have been forwarded to the Bureau for translation."

The file on me ends with a page of my physical characteristics and my relatives in Japan and the United States. The very last word on the last page is "PENDING." I presume the report was written in September 1944 because it mentions the fact that I was leaving Chicago that month, which means that Mr. Orton didn't write the report until three months after the interrogation. My months of worry and of not writing in my diary had been for naught, because obviously there was no urgency involved in handling my case. In fact, if I hadn't visited him on September 7 to request that my possessions be returned, he might not have written the report for several months more.

Carleton

My experience at the Central YMCA College proved that it was possible to earn college credits even in a skyscraper in a metropolis. But I still hoped to attend classes on a traditional campus—with green lawns and trees surrounding ivy-covered buildings.

I wrote to the Student Relocation Committee in Philadelphia, inquiring about a school that met *my* requirements, to which I might be able to transfer. The committee's reply was that for my purposes Carleton College at Northfield, Minnesota, was to be recommended. This judgment was based on a survey of small, coeducational liberal arts colleges in the United States.

The academic level of the faculty and the size of the library were the major criteria used, by which Carleton ranked highest in the Midwest. Rated likewise were Swarthmore College on the East Coast and Pomona College on the West Coast.

My letter to Carleton elicited a reply from the college's director of admissions, Donald Klinefelter. He advised me to visit the college's representative stationed in Chicago, Dr. Benjamin Van Riper.

The letter was welcome because it showed that Carleton was willing to consider accepting me and that it had an office in downtown Chicago where I could present myself to speak to someone directly.

On June 1, 1944, I found Dr. Van Riper manning his office alone in a building at 209 South State Street. The moment I saw him, I was struck by the fact that he would pass for a twin of John L. Lewis, the feisty president of the United Mine Workers of America, whose portrait I had seen frequently in the newspapers in connection with strikes.

Any resemblance between Dr. Van Riper and the trade union leader, however, was confined to their appearances, accentuated by bushy eyebrows. When I announced that I had been directed to his office, Dr. Van Riper stepped forward from behind his desk, all smiles.

"I would like to transfer to Carleton."

"Well, that's an excellent idea," he said, with particular emphasis on the word "excellent."

"Let me show you what our college looks like," he continued, pointing to pictures on the walls. "This is the general view of the campus." He started out with a bird's-eye view of the campus with buildings scattered sparsely on a large tract of land with trees. "This is . . . ," he went on, seemingly oblivious of the question of my qualifications for admission. I could not believe my ears. This was the college ranked highest in the Midwest for academics? How could Carleton—or any college for that matter—take just *anybody*?

Becoming slightly apprehensive, I interrupted.

"By the way, I am an alien."

"What? Canadian?" Dr. Van Riper shot back unconcernedly.

"No. An ay-lee-an. Enemy alien. I came from Japan three years ago."

"Oh, that doesn't make any difference," he said most affably and with obvious sincerity. "Carleton has always welcomed foreign students."

Later I learned the basis of this statement. In 1937, Frank B. Kellogg, the former U.S. Secretary of State and one of the architects of the Pact of Paris of 1928 that was meant to outlaw war, gave half a million dollars to Carleton to establish the Frank B. Kellogg Foundation. Funds from the foundation created the Department of

International Relations at the college and helped it invite students from abroad. By the early 1940s there were 11 to 15 such students on the campus each year.

I described my college career of one year, along with the number of credit hours I would have gained between then and September. As far as Dr. Van Riper was concerned, my admission at the college was a foregone conclusion. He gave me an application form, which I was to mail to Mr. Klinefelter at Northfield.

After that, Dr. Van Riper became even more friendly. He was a retired professor of psychology from Carleton, I learned. He had a son my age in the Army Air Corps, learning to fly. The college official took great delight in telling me that during a recent training program, his son thought he had done "pretty good" in bringing his aircraft to a rendezvous "*only* two minutes late."

"But he was bawled out for not being on time," the happy father chortled.

He decided to close shop for the day and drove me to East Sixty-first Street on his way home.

On July 5, I received a formal letter of acceptance from the college in Northfield, for the academic year beginning in mid-September. My great-aunt was willing to pay for the tuition, which was close to that of Princeton, then considered to be one of the most expensive colleges in the United States.

Northfield in September 1944 was a quiet town, with a population of 4,500. It was best known as the site of a disastrous attempt by the James Gang to rob the town bank in 1876. The ordinary peacetime enrollment of the college had been four hundred "boys" and four hundred "girls." In that particular war year, however, the enrollment was at a peak of abnormality, consisting almost entirely of women—eight hundred of them—with a woefully small male representation of about sixty. This explained why Dr. Van Riper had been so enthusiastic about my interest in his college. In fact, for this particular year, the whole male contingent of the student body resided at a single dormitory, named Margaret Evans Hall (normally a women's dormitory, as the name suggested).

The rest of the sixty-odd "boys" were mostly real boys—males under draft age. The others were 4-Fs—draft-exempted because of physical handicaps—and foreign students, including one from Japan, myself.

On one of the very first days of my presence on the campus, a member of the faculty spotted me at a distance of about fifty feet, raised his arm, and said heartily: "*Saludos amigo!*" Obviously, he mistook me for one of the several Latin American students on the campus. But I appreciated this friendliness, which seemed to symbolize the family-like atmosphere of the college.

I found Carleton truly like a big family, because practically everyone knew everyone else. And within a few weeks, practically everyone knew me or knew of me. Although the students expressed interest in my situation and background, not one of them made reference to the fact that my country was at war with theirs. The college community was much more focused on campus life itself than on the war. Furthermore, as I explained to them, I had come to America not knowing war was imminent. The war had no more to do with my studies than it did with theirs. Like all Americans I had encountered thus far, they were simply too discreet to bring up a subject that they thought would embarrass me.

Inasmuch as I had taken to Carleton forty-four credit hours and eighty-seven grade credits from Central YMCA College, I started out as a fairly advanced sophomore. As such, I was in a position to observe with detachment the curious custom of hazing, in which upperclassmen treated freshmen students with seeming contempt and ridicule but with no real malice.

Hazing of freshmen was theoretically forbidden, according to a letter from the president of the Men's League, distributed among the frosh. But it said there were a number of "traditions" to be observed. One was that frosh were required to wear green caps outdoors except on Sundays and when they were off campus. Another was that they must remain seated after a chapel service, a compulsory semiweekly religious program, until all others had left.

Aside from the written "traditions," there was one other mild form of hazing: An upperclassman seeing a freshman walking on campus gave the command of "Button!" This required the freshman to put the books he was carrying on his head—over the button of his beanie—and walk backward until the command was revoked.

This was only for boys. For women the only visible form of hazing was that one day during the first semester, all freshman women wore grotesque makeup applied by their elders, to the consternation of new male students on the campus. According to my brief experience in a college in Osaka and my general knowledge of the country, hazing had no parallel in Japan. The strange American custom, therefore, amused and bemused me.

In the men's dormitory many of the students, particularly young ones, found me an object of intense curiosity, and my room served as a hall for nearly nightly bull sessions. One of the early, inevitable questions was: "Kiyo, do you know jujutsu?"

Because my middle school martial arts training was in kendo, I had never studied judo formally. The only experience I had was the practice I attempted in the gymnasium of the YMCA on LaSalle Street in downtown Chicago with instructions I found in a book.

Reluctant to disappoint the boys, I would say, "Yes, a little," which reflected more my honesty than my modesty. And a request for a demonstration always followed.

We would adjourn to the living room of the dormitory, where I removed cushions from the sofas and couches and laid them on the floor. A few elementary throws were sufficient to impress the youngsters, to whom judo was apparently a mysterious Oriental art of felling an adversary without the brute force of a hard fist.

Almost unavoidably, I established a reputation as a judo expert. When the Men's League was planning a recreation program in the den in the dormitory on the night of March 10, Saturday, 1945, a member of the program committee thought of a number featuring a judo demonstration. And I agreed to participate in it.

Following songs, a French can-can by boys with gear they had borrowed from female students, and other performances, came my number.

John McKenzie, a cadet on leave from West Point to study at Carleton, was on stage, wearing hideous makeup designed to make him look like a drunkard.

"We now present a great judo expert direct from Japan—Kiyoaki Murata!" he barked. My partner, who also served as master of ceremonies, had wanted me to wear something exotic. Since I had no such costume, I wore a brown cashmere bathrobe I had inherited from my great-uncle, intended as a substitute for a kimono. We had spread a wrestling mat on the wooden floor.

"Anyone who wants to have an arm broken, please step forward," said John sadistically. Silence.

"Since there is no one with enough courage to take part in this show," he said with feigned disgust, "I will have to do it myself." We followed our script, in which I was to use three different techniques in succession to throw John as he "attacked" me.

The first was *ashibarai*, tripping of a foot, which sent the West Pointer, at least five inches taller than I, to the floor. John came at me again, acting like a humiliated drunk. This time I used a *haraigoshi* (hip throw), and he landed on his back. With a grimace, he got back on his feet again. Now he employed an exaggerated swing of his long arm. I pivoted on my right foot to catch his body on my back, seized his right arm with my hands, and, using his forward momentum to my advantage, threw him over my head. Each time there was applause from the audience, which was largely female and sprinkled with several members of the faculty. The event further spread my spurious reputation as a judo expert.

Another memorable event for me at Carleton came in November 1944. At the college, compulsory chapel services were held on Tuesdays and Fridays, when a member of the faculty or an invited guest addressed the assembly. Friday, November 17, however, was different. Three foreign students were asked to speak to mark International Student Day, observed to commemorate the students massacred by Nazis in Prague.

I was one of the three. The assignment made me nervous because it was to be my first public address anywhere and, furthermore, I was to speak in English.

For the subject, I chose my favorite theme of those years: the problems of East and West. I stepped up to the chapel rostrum and began my speech.

"It is not true that 'never the twain shall meet.' They have already met," I said. "But the two have not yet found a common formula for coexistence. The mission of our generation is to establish a peace in which all the peoples of the world can live and prosper together. For that, we must first of all know and understand each other. Ignorance is not bliss; ignorance is a danger. That's the reason why I came to America."

My brief address was met with great applause. Later, in the afternoon astronomy class, one of the students said to me, "They should have given you all of the time. Would you speak longer if we asked you to?"

This was one of the friendliest of the women students at the friendly college, Agnes Parker from Chicago. We soon became close companions. I treasured our innocent friendship, once again proud that my Confucian ideals were not being compromised.

Among the faculty were two refugees from Europe. One was Moritz Julius Bonn, a professor of economics, who was probably the only member of the Carleton faculty who rated a mention in *Webster's Biographical Dictionary* (1943). He was described as a "German economist" and author of "works chiefly on world economy and politics."

As distinguished a scholar as he might have been, however, Professor Bonn was (like Thorstein Veblen, the most celebrated alumnus of Carleton College) not a good lecturer. For one thing, he was handicapped by his heavy German accent. Yet, as a human being, he was a total stranger to intellectual arrogance.

On the morning of November 2, 1944, I fell in with him on my way to the center of campus. I had finally grown accustomed to the American practice of walking abreast of one's teachers. Eager to make use of the precious opportunity to pick the scholar's brains, I posed a question that was most appropriate as far as my scanty knowledge of economics and the professor's background were concerned.

"Did Germany really need *Lebensraum*?"

Professor Bonn benignly smiled and said, "Do we know what *Lebensraum* is?"

In prewar Japan this concept, propounded by Nazi leaders, was sometimes cited in reference to Japan's military adventurism in Asia.

"I have a vague notion of it," I said.

Professor Bonn's answer was characteristically laconic.

"So does Hitler."

Then he launched into a very conscientious exposition of the national economic problems of Germany until we reached the college post office building, where we parted.

On the day when we were to have the final exam in Dr. Bonn's class, we sat expectantly with blue books on the desks. To our surprise, he came into the classroom without anything that looked like sheets of paper bearing exam questions.

With a smile, the teacher told the puzzled class, "The question for the examination is this: Write about any of the things we discussed in class during the semester."

This was somehow characteristic of the great scholar. I used two blue books to write all I could. A week later, he returned to the class and began passing out the blue books.

"Murata," he said when my turn came. Instead of simply handing me my exam paper, he was about to say something.

"What?" I wondered, standing before the teacher.

"What you wrote," he said, "is all wrong. But you thought very independently. Therefore, I gave you a very good grade."

Hopefully I opened the first page to find a mere B.

Back at the campus after the Christmas–New Year holidays, Agnes related to me an interesting episode. She had told her friends in Chicago about Carleton and the fact that one of her new friends was a student from Japan. Her Chicago friends told her to "be careful because he might stab you in the back."

"I laughed," she said. I enjoyed the story enormously.

In the second semester, I took a class taught by the other refugee member of the faculty, Dr. Hans Weigert. An associate professor of geography, Dr. Weigert had received recognition in the United States after publishing a book titled *Generals and Geographers*, a critique of Nazi *geopolitik*. The class I took was called Geography of the Far East.

As Allied victories accumulated, media attention shifted from battles themselves to the question of what to do after the enemy nations surrendered. From late 1944, I had been reading various essays by American leaders and intellectuals about what to do with the Emperor system in postwar Japan. Most views favored abolition of the imperial institution on the premise that Emperor worship was the source of Japan's military expansionism.

Representative of this notion was an article by Sun Fo in the October 1944 issue of *Foreign Affairs*. In this tract entitled "Mikado Must Go," the son of Sun Yat-sen and a prominent leader of Nationalist China advocated destroying the "Japanese myth that deified the Mikado."

The spring of 1945 saw increased discussions of the problem. Owen Lattimore's *Solution in Asia* received probably greater attention than Sun Fo's article. The American expert on China proposed that "[the Emperor] and all males eligible for the throne by Japanese rules of succession and adoption should be interned, preferably in China but under the supervision of a United Nations commission."

At about the same time, I was amazed to read in a newspaper an interview with one K. K. Kawakami, a longtime Japanese resident in the United States. Kawakami stated that he favored bombing the Imperial Palace in Tokyo as a way to end the war.

The grounds for this suggestion were absurd. Kawakami said the Emperor was known in Japanese as "Son of Heaven." Therefore if bombs should fall from heaven to destroy his palace—and possibly his own person—that would demolish the popular belief and hasten Japan's surrender. I was shocked that Kawakami should consider his own countrymen to be so primitive and superstitious.

I was also mystified that this particular man had recommended such a course of action. Through the 1930s the very same Kawakami had written extensively in English to explain, if not to apologize for, Japan's Asia policy. His 1933 book, *Manchukuo: Child of Conflict*, based on his on-the-spot fact-gathering, for instance, eloquently spoke of the validity and possibility of existence of what was in fact a puppet regime of Japan.

Meanwhile, views that basically differed from those of Sun Fo, Lattimore, and the new Kawakami were being expressed by a few Americans, most prominently Undersecretary of State Joseph Grew. The former ambassador to Japan maintained that the Emperor should be spared to serve as the only stabilizing force in postwar Japan.

The question of what to do with the Emperor system after Japan's capitulation was also discussed in Professor David Bryn-Jones's seminar in international relations at Carleton. One of the students in the class contributed an essay on the subject to *The Carletonian* in its March 24 issue. In the column entitled "The CSR" (Committee on Social Relations), whose mission was to "clarify and formulate the fundamental issues of our day," she essentially followed the line proposed by Lattimore in rejecting the Emperor as "divine ruler" while waving aside Grew's position.

This compelled me to rebut the article. I felt I could not go on record as having failed to do so. This did not mean, however, that I had a clear notion of the shape of things to come in Japan. What I knew was that the persons who were blithely prescribing policies for a future Japan were handicapped by a lack of pertinent information.

I went to see Tek Konsberg, the student editor of the campus publication, who welcomed my offer to write. The next issue of *The Carletonian*, dated April 14, 1945, carried my contribution of approximately 1,300 words under the heading of "Emperor: To Be or Not To Be." Tek prefaced my piece with his editor's note: "Although CSR has stated its position on this problem, we welcome the following expression of opinion by one who is interested in, and familiar with the subject."

One of the key points I tried to present was the semantic confusion about the status of the Emperor. I did this by pointing out the traditional mistranslation of the term *kami* as "god" or, worse still, "God" in English. I rejected the then popular view that the Emperor system was the fountainhead of Japan's military aggression. I wrote that if war could start from "a single factor of such a simple nature, we could have established a perpetual peace many generations ago, and millions of our fellow men need not be killed and maimed today.

"But, unfortunately the causes of war are highly complex, and human intelligence is as yet too inadequate to cope with such a difficult problem."

The Emperor of Japan "is a symbol of the state," I wrote, and the concept of state is superimposed on that of the people. A Japanese soldier who is willing to die for the Emperor is in reality sacrificing himself for his compatriots or his fatherland.

Therefore, I argued, the "physical obliteration" of the Emperor would serve no constructive purpose for Japan or any other country. It would only cause his successor to be enthroned and further stir the fighting spirit of the nation.

To illustrate my thesis, I said: "We can destroy concrete entities, but we cannot destroy abstractions in the same manner. Is it not a plain fact that even if bombs can demolish the statue of Nathan Hale on the campus of Yale University, his spirit will not be effaced from the mind of every patriotic American?"

Judging from what happened in the post-surrender years, the Grew school of thought evidently prevailed in Washington. In the

American-drafted postwar Constitution of Japan, the Emperor is defined as "the symbol of the state and of the unity of the people" (Article 1). The United States government also successfully shielded him against attempts by its Allies to prosecute him for war crimes. Having been shorn of all political powers, the Emperor of Japan has remained a symbol of popular sovereignty through the postwar decades.

Toward the end of the term, Dr. Weigert asked me if I would be willing to spend a session with his students in the Japanese geography class he was giving at the Twin Cities Campus of the University of Minnesota. His students were cadets studying under the Army Specialized Training Program (ASTP), which I was told trained young officers primarily for occupation duties to be carried out in Japan after surrender.

I consented because I could see nothing treasonous about imparting what I knew about Japan to the ASTP students. As of May 1945, the war appeared to be coming to an end in the Allied Powers' favor. And Dr. Weigert's students were most likely to become engaged not in wartime intelligence but in postwar life in Japan.

After announcing my visit to his class, Dr. Weigert told me he was worried. "They all thought you were a spy. They could not believe that a student from Japan could be studying in this country now." Dr. Weigert was concerned about how the Army students would react to me when I appeared before them; he thought they might be hostile.

I was not surprised by the reaction of the students and of my teacher. But I said, "Please don't worry," confident that Dr. Weigert's misgivings were out of place.

The day was to be June 1, when I planned to leave Northfield to spend the summer in Chicago. I could leave Minneapolis by train after speaking to the ASTP class.

I faced about two hundred khaki-uniformed young men of my age, filling an amphitheater classroom of the University of Minnesota in the Twin Cities.

"Let me introduce Kiyoaki Murata from Japan . . ."

There was thunderous applause.

"You have never given *me* such a big hand before," the professor said, feigning jealousy to the merry laughter of the class.

I noticed a stack of sheets of paper, lists of five questions from each student. They wanted to obtain knowledge about Japan from a live source to supplement the information they had received from their classes and books. Obviously, I could not answer all of the thousand questions. So Dr. Weigert had selected a smaller number, and began to read the questions one by one.

"Do Japanese farmers eat bread at all?" was the first.

"Generally speaking, no," I replied, adding that their "staple food" was rice and they also ate fish, vegetables, and some meat.

Dr. Weigert asked the students: "Did you all understand the answer?"

Somewhat to my surprise, laughter drowned out the yeses.

"What do young men in rural Japan do in the way of recreation?" was the second question. This was far tougher than the first because in the land of asceticism that Japan was in the 1930s, recreation was not one of the most important elements of life. I mentioned seasonal *sumo* tournaments held on public school grounds and a few other similar items.

After about the fifteenth question, the bell rang and the first hour was over for an intermission. I was immediately surrounded by a dozen students who did not want to waste the ten minutes. They showered me with questions.

When the second session was over, again I was besieged by eager seekers of knowledge. Then one of them said, "We are studying Japanese in other classes. If you have time, we would like you to come to our room so that we can learn more from you."

I agreed because I had nothing to do until the night train. As we ate in the cafeteria, one of the boys said, "Did you know why we all laughed when Dr. Weigert asked us if we understood your answer?"

"No," I said, glad the subject had been brought up.

"Because your English was much better than his!"

The moment I entered their dormitory room, which several men shared, my eyes were riveted to a Rising Sun flag on the wall with inscriptions of Japanese names. It was the kind of flag each young man of Japan, called to the colors, received from his friends, who autographed it to wish the recipient good luck on the front. But this flag was clean and did not seem to be a souvenir from the Pacific theater of war. For one thing, the names and the calligraphy did not appear authentic.

"That's our Hinomaru" (Rising Sun Flag), explained one of the young men to resolve my wonderment. "Those names are ours."

"My name is Shoulder," said he, pointing to a single ideograph, which was indeed the word *kata* (shoulder).

"This is me," said another, pointing to a set of two characters which read *sanpo* (stroll). He said his name was Stroll. Likewise, all other names were deciphered for me.

"Please read us a story," they said, handing me the Japanese textbook they used in their language class. Their choice was "Momotaro," the popular Japanese folk tale about a boy who is born out of a large *momo* (peach) and reared by an old childless couple. The peach-boy goes to the Devils' Islands to chastise the horned devils for having harassed human beings. Though we were unaware of it, this particular story had taken on military overtones in Japan because of its supposed parallels with Japan's wartime situation. In fact, during the Occupation, GHQ actually banned the story altogether, replacing it with one about Momojiro, presumably Momotaro's younger brother. To us, however, the story was nothing more than an innocent and enjoyable folk tale.

Toward the evening, I stood in the chow line again as a guest of one of the boys. Later, others joined us in a restaurant in town to help me kill time until I boarded the 10:30 P.M. train.

As we sat in a booth, one of the young men jovially greeted a young, plump waitress, "Hi, Nickie!" Then he asked me, "Do you know why we call her Nickie?"

"No, why?"

"The real name we gave her is 'Niku,' which as you know means 'flesh.' So we call her Nickie. And she seems to like it too." We all had a big laugh over the linguistic prank.

After hours of friendly chat, I was to head for the station. Representing his colleagues who had to be back at their billet to observe the curfew, the fellow who had signed his name as Sanpo on the Rising Sun flag walked me to the station. The enjoyable encounter with the ASTP students proved that I, not Dr. Weigert, had been correct in anticipating their reaction to me.

Chapter
14

"WAR IS OVER"

After completing my first year at Carleton College at the end of May 1945, I was to spend the summer months usefully by earning credits at the University of Chicago. By that time, the Army ban against Japanese students for security reasons related to the Manhattan Project had been lifted. When I applied for the summer term, I was accepted because I had passed the aptitude and placement tests in 1943.

At the university, I registered for three courses. I also found a job as a busboy in the Commons dining hall, the large cafeteria for students and faculty. Kitchen work was becoming quite familiar to me.

I spent my off hours at Brent House, a church-established facility for helping students in Chicago meet foreign students. There I met Evelyn Mannheim, a woman who was to become a close friend that summer. I was attracted by her personality and physical charm, and supposed that she found me novel because of my background.

One of the traits I liked about her was that she seldom wore heavy makeup because, she said, she did not wish to look "gaudy."

When she said this, I responded with what I thought was a compliment: "You look pretty without anything on."

I did not realize this was a blooper until several months later, back at Carleton, when I related this bit of conversation to Agnes. She said, "Evelyn must have slapped you when you said that."

As news of the war drew on, it was easy to sense that the end was near. Just as I was wondering how Mr. Judge was faring in his study of Japanese, and if he would have to see combat, I began to receive APO letters from him—now Lieutenant Judge—sent from "somewhere in the Pacific." In July, I received one from "Western Pacific," which contained what appeared to be a coded message. It would have escaped the attention of any censor—aside from the question of whether the hidden message endangered Army security.

Mr. Judge wrote, "Here, *uchi* is used oftener than *watashi*."

He was in Okinawa!

One of the first-person singular pronouns in standard Japanese is *watashi*. But in the western part of Japan, the dialect counterpart used by women is *uchi*. If Mr. Judge was in contact with persons who used this word, he could only have been somewhere in the Japanese islands, or more specifically, Okinawa.

The Battle of Okinawa had begun on April 1, when U.S. forces landed on the main island, where the capital of Naha was located, and had come to an end on June 23. I presumed Mr. Judge was using his Japanese in communicating with the civilian population that included women. I was overwhelmed by the fact that my American teacher was now thousands of miles closer to my own home than I was.

An inspiration—though based on wishful thinking and ignorance—hit me. I wrote a brief letter in Japanese to my parents and put it in a small envelope, addressing the envelope with my father's name and address as I would do in Japan. Then I enclosed it in my letter to Lt. Judge at his APO address.

My hope was that if this letter to my father should ever be—I did not know how—inserted into the Japanese postal service system, it would not fail to reach him. I knew any letter with insufficient postage and without a return address was sure to be delivered—for collecting the postage.

Toward the evening of August 5, I was visiting Evelyn at one of the dormitories for women. She showed me the evening paper with the front-page news about Hiroshima having been "atomized" with 300,000 casualties.

"Japan must surrender quickly. Otherwise . . . ," Evelyn said thoughtfully. Back at the dormitory of the Chicago Theological Seminary, which made rooms available to any student during the summer, I found many divinity students incensed by the use of this powerful new weapon on civilians. I was surprised to hear one of them say, "This is unforgivable." Examples of Americans criticizing the actions of their own government still startled me.

But Japan did not surrender that day, or even in the following few days, after a second bomb was dropped. On August 7, the first public reports on the development of the atomic bomb began to appear. Reading them, I realized with a shock that this had been the very "secret military project" that had barred my admission to Chicago.

Starting on August 11, I was reassigned to work in a section of the facility that served exclusively the ASTP students who were studying the Japanese language—the same program as those at the Twin Cities Campus in Minnesota and other major universities.

On that morning, I got up as usual at 6:30 A.M. in my room in the seminary dormitory. I ran to the Commons and set up the table. Promptly at 7:00 A.M., the doors were opened and the hungry young men filed in.

Pitchers full of coffee and cocoa were passed around and milk jugs emptied and refilled. As the boys munched toast and sipped beverages, one student, a latecomer, dashed in.

"It's all over!" he shouted breathlessly, holding up a newspaper extra above his head.

"WAR IS OVER," the banner headline said. An excited babble filled the room, and the students scurried out as soon as they finished their breakfast.

The headline on the extra turned out to be somewhat premature. Japan had informed the Allied Powers through the Swiss government that she was prepared to accept the terms of the Potsdam Proclamation if the Emperor's status would be left intact. The Allied

Powers agreed on condition that the Emperor be "subject to" the Supreme Commander of the Allied Powers.

After the first shift of the 150 ASTP students left, the tables were wet with spilled coffee and cluttered with bread crumbs.

"Usually they are much better mannered," one of my co-workers said apologetically, because it was my first day there. "They were too excited today." She was correct. The next day, the students were back to their usual mannerliness.

At 6:00 P.M. on August 14, President Harry S. Truman announced in a special radio message that Japan had capitulated unconditionally to the Allied Powers. My ingenuous reaction was that of joy and relief because, I felt, people no longer had to be killed.

Having observed war from the other side—more objectively than my compatriots at home who were fed government propaganda—I had had no illusions about Japan's being ultimately defeated, as I had told the assistant district attorney in Chicago. I felt life in Japan after surrender would not be easy because of the shortage of goods and food. But it would not be worse than the wanton waste of human life war had meant.

I was not concerned about any of my immediate relatives getting killed because I knew none would be in the service and our home was in a rural area not subject to bombing. But my middle school classmates were another matter. I had often wondered about them and how many might be dead at the war's end.

The university was to hold a special prayer meeting in the Rockefeller Memorial chapel, the Gothic landmark on the campus, at eight o'clock. I wanted to be present and headed for the chapel. Then I returned to my room to pick up a camera.

As an enemy alien, I was forbidden to possess a camera, which was contraband. But according to my own interpretation of federal regulations, I was not forbidden to *use* a camera that belonged to someone else. As a matter of fact, I did have such a camera—one an American friend had allowed me to use on a semi-permanent basis. I had taken pictures of my friends at picnics, and so forth, including a particularly memorable one of an anti-Japanese slogan on a mail truck. I used it on that day to photograph the service from the balcony of the chapel as no one else did.

One sultry evening several days later, I was sitting on a bench near Cobb Hall with Evelyn. A column of ASTP students came marching by with books under their arms, obviously headed for a night class of Japanese. The column came to a halt in front of us. When the men fell out, a score of them surrounded our bench.

"*Konbanwa*" (good evening), one of them said.

"Hello," I replied in English.

"Do you speak Japanese?" the student ventured uncertainly, half disappointed that I did not reply in Japanese.

"Yes," I said with some hesitation because I had not spoken the language for quite some time. "Do you?"

"I speak Texan Japanese," another said.

"Do you boys still have to study Japanese even after the cessation of hostilities?"

"I guess so. We may be shipped to Japan for occupation duties. But I wanna go home."

"*Anata wa kireina hito desu*," one addressed Evelyn, trying out a Japanese sentence he had learned in class.

"What does that mean?" she asked me, half impressed and half curious.

"It means 'You are a beautiful person,'" I translated.

"Please say something in Japanese," another insisted, anxious for me to speak Japanese to see if he would understand it and if what they learned in class was intelligible to a native speaker.

I hesitated for a few moments and said, "*Kyo wa taihen atsui desu*" (It's very hot today). Though I had tried to be as articulate as I could, the Army linguists all cocked their heads.

"*Atsui desu*," I tried again. They finally caught on.

"Oh, *aTSUI desu*!"

I had pronounced the word as "Atsui," with the stress on the first syllable, the way people in my home region do, which differed from the accentuation of standard Japanese spoken in Tokyo and its surrounding areas.

"I am glad you are learning standard Japanese," I said to reassure them that it was my wrong accent that had befuddled them.

Now the students had to go to class. Reluctantly they went into Cobb Hall and then upstairs. From the windows several waved at us as if they envied me for being able to relax on a campus bench while they had to grind away at a tough foreign language.

Then suddenly, one of them came running downstairs.

"My name is Jerome Wodinsky," he said breathlessly. "I want to keep in touch with you. I want to practice speaking Japanese."

The debilitating war came to an end for Japan on August 15, 1945. In an unprecedented radio broadcast at noon on that day, the Emperor told his subjects to lay down arms because he had "resolved to pave the way for a grand peace for all the generations to come, by enduring the unendurable and suffering what is unsufferable."

As if to add insult to injury, the Empire was hit by two disastrous typhoons in the autumn—on September 18 and in early October, which further devastated the war-ravaged land. In Hyogo Prefecture, a major rice-producing region of the country, the crop for the year had been reduced by one-half. Kawai Mura was one of the worst-hit areas because on October 8 the Kako River overflowed, inundating the rice paddies and homes, including my parents'.

By October 30, Tuesday, the village was slowly recovering from the havoc wrought by the flood. Farmers were out in the paddies to harvest what they could of the rice, whose stalks had been lying on the now-dried mud.

At about two o'clock, my parents were visited by the young stationmaster—and the only station hand—of Kawai Nishi Station, located about five hundred yards away. It was from this station that I had boarded a diesel-engine train to head for America a little more than four years earlier.

Having pedaled his bicycle as fast as he could, he was still panting—and he seemed tense—when he told my mother: "They telephoned me from Kakogawa Station to say that an American is coming by the next train—an American officer—to see Mr. Murata. They want someone to be at the station—someone who understands English."

He left, after making certain his message had been digested and repeating "by the next train at 3:09."

The message struck the household like a thunderbolt. An American officer was coming to see my father! But what for?

Following the surrender ceremony on the *USS Missouri* on September 2, General Douglas MacArthur, the Supreme Commander for the Allied Powers (SCAP), set up general headquarters in Tokyo. And the headquarters—also known as SCAP—relentlessly went about converting militarist Japan into a democracy by issuing one directive after another. One of these was the initiation of War Crimes trials.

There was a general fear among Japanese about these trials, and any news about an American officer coming to speak to an individual had an ominous ring to it. But my father had always been a schoolteacher and had retired in August for health reasons after serving as a headmaster for more than ten years. How could he possibly be interrogated as a war crimes suspect?

Regardless, his presence at the station seemed mandatory. Whether he could speak English or not was beside the point. He was to meet this important caller—whoever it might be. So he changed into a business suit. He decided to take my eight-year-old brother Kazushige along, to give the young boy the chance to meet an officer of the occupying United States Army.

The two headed for the station on foot. In the meantime, my mother replaced her *monpe*, the wartime work clothes for women, with a kimono and she tidied the house as best she could in the short time she had. Fortunately my elder sister Akiko, now twenty-five, was visiting my parents with her infant daughter, so she was able to help my mother and my other sister Masako, now eighteen.

The train arrived on time. Among the passengers who got off at Kawai Nishi was a single American—in Army uniform. My father stepped forward and before he could attempt to compose a sentence in English, the American said, "*Murata-san desuka? Watashi Judge chui desu. Kiyoaki no tomodachi desu*" (Mr. Murata? I am Lt. Judge— a friend of Kiyoaki's).

Instantly, it all made sense to my father. A feeling of relief and gratification overwhelmed him. He recalled that in my letters of the summer of 1941, I had occasionally mentioned a "very kind American teacher" at Drew School by the name of Jajji. This was the famous Mr. Judge, and he had come all the way from Tokyo—or, as a matter of fact, from America—to Kawai Mura to tell him about his son.

As Mr. Judge related how he had met me in San Francisco and how I was doing in the United States, he saw my father brush aside a tear or two—contrary to what he had been told in his ASTP classes, that the Japanese were a stoic people who did not show emotions.

The curious threesome—an American Army officer, a middleaged Japanese and a young boy—ambled down the country road that cut through the rice paddies. The farmers all stopped harvesting rice stalks and gawked at the first American they had ever laid eyes on. Indeed, no American had ever set foot on the soil of Kawai Mura in its thousand-year history. And the American, to the surprise of the farmers, bowed to each of them.

Arriving home, my father triumphantly announced to his family: "The visitor is Kiyoaki's teacher!"

My mother rushed to the entrance hall.

"*Oh, Okaasan, watashi Kiyoaki no sensei,*" the visitor introduced himself. (Oh, Mother, I am Kiyoaki's teacher.)

Then the lieutenant produced from his jacket pocket his "credentials" to prove beyond a shadow of a doubt the authenticity of his status in relation to me: two recent letters from me and three photographs. The pictures showed me as a fully grown young man, looking somewhat "American" by my glasses, haircut, and clothes, but nonetheless unmistakably my parents' son, and obviously in good health and in high spirits. Reading the letters and looking at the photographs, my mother alternately wept and laughed with joy.

Watching the ecstatic family, Lt. Judge mused over the events of the past four years. One day in July 1941, a Japanese boy had walked into his English class in San Francisco. He found the new pupil strange not only in his appearance but also in his outlook on life. His encounter with the student caused him to take enormous interest in Japan, a faraway country of which he then knew hardly anything.

It was because of the war neither he—nor I—anticipated in those months, that he was now in Japan visiting the home where the Japanese youth had grown up. He was, furthermore, now speaking to the youth's parents in their own language.

Lt. Judge's visit unraveled a major mystery that had puzzled my parents since October 8. On that day a few weeks earlier—when the Kako River had overflowed—my parents received a mysterious letter. The envelope was addressed to my father and the handwriting was unmistakably mine. Inside was my letter, which did not explain how it would be delivered to them. But it did carry a vital message: I was out of the "detention center" and now studying in a college, moving forward to my goal. In fact, I was doing all right. There was nothing to worry about.

On the obverse side of the envelope, however, was the name of a total stranger, one Hikoji Otsuki, whose address made no sense because the man lived in Iruma, Saitama Prefecture, north of Tokyo. My parents knew nobody in that part of the country. But the letter carried the required postage.

This was the letter of July 28 that I had sent to Mr. Judge in Okinawa, asking him to insert it into the Japanese postal system. He had obliged, though not in Okinawa, but as soon as it became feasible for him to do so—after arriving on Japan's main island following the surrender. He did so with the assistance of a Japanese Army liaison officer he worked with at a military facility he was assigned to as an interpreter.

In his letter of late September, postmarked October 1, Lt. Judge wrote to me that he had mailed my letter from Iruma and that he hoped to see my family before November 1.

His plan, however, had sounded unrealistic to me. Judging by news from post-surrender Japan, the whole situation there was chaotic. People were in a daze and the transportation system was in serious disarray. Neither the American occupier nor the Japanese were certain of what to expect of the other. Under such circumstances, I could not visualize Mr. Judge taking a journey over a distance of more than 350 miles by himself to the heart of Honshu, the main island, to see my parents, sisters, and brother.

But Mr. Judge had meant it. Initially, he wrote later, he thought of flying, but "inclement weather" ruled it out. The alternative was driving, but he "had smashed up his jeep." The only choice left was the train.

His westward journey was an adventure through wilderness. He had to inquire at many points along the way how to get to his destination. After an overnight stay in Osaka, he reached Kakogawa, a junction point where he had been told to transfer to a branch line. There, upon his inquiry, station hands held a long conference to determine at which station the American should get off, because there were three in Kawai Mura. Finally, they decided it should be the middle one, Kawai Nishi.

But then, there was a three-hour wait for him until the next train left for Kawai Nishi and beyond at 2:17.

Having no alternative, the lieutenant decided to kill time by strolling through town. During his walk, he came upon a middle school, of the kind I had attended until the spring of 1941. A great novelty to youngsters and local people, he attracted "at least three hundred children," by his no doubt somewhat exaggerated estimate, who followed him to the station. There he was surrounded again, this time by a crowd of very curious adults. The crowd showered him with questions, which the American tried to answer in Japanese during the twenty minutes before boarding the train.

When the train came, station hands set up a special seat for Lt. Judge in the baggage car next to the locomotive's tender. When the engine pulling a few cars and a larger number of boxcars puffed out on its northward journey, the Kakogawa stationmaster cranked the handle of the railway telephone to raise Kawai Nishi Station. He announced that the train due in about fifty minutes was carrying a very important passenger, whose destination should not be far from the station. The Kawai Nishi stationmaster should notify one Mr. Murata.

The accommodation for the American on the train was designed to spare him from being stared at or questioned by other passengers. But when the train stopped at Hioka, a few miles north of Kakogawa, someone in the waiting room of the station house spotted the unusual passenger and called him to the attention of others. All seemed entranced by the sight of an American officer on a local train, and gathered around the door for a closer look.

Exactly the same thing happened at Kanno, the second stop, and so on until his destination. But Lt. Judge was just as curious about his surroundings as the onlookers were about him.

Kawai Nishi was the seventh station from Kakogawa. After the train passed the sixth stop, he glued his eyes to the window with enormous interest in the area that he knew was his pupil's home village. Finally, the train ground to a halt at a very small station, where an elderly gentleman and a young boy were waiting for him.

At the house, though my mother had wondered if the American might not be able to sit on the floor as Japanese did and offered him a chair, Lt. Judge said he preferred to sit down on the tatami floor. He removed his shoes and went into the guest room to which he was led. There, he was seated in the place of honor with the *tokonoma* alcove at his back. My whole family, including the visiting Akiko, joined him in the room.

At first, they were incredulous about what was happening. They tried to entertain the visitor. But soon they found themselves being entertained by his stories of me in America. He told them, for instance: "Kiyoaki was always studying. He never had time for play. He was always very serious.

"When he walked with me on a sidewalk," he told them, "he always walked a few steps behind me."

My mother showed him family albums containing photographs of me in infancy, childhood, and so on.

Mr. Judge suggested that my family write letters, which he would mail from Tokyo to me at Carleton.

So my mother wrote: "It's like a dream. What a strange twist of fate. Your teacher is such a kind person and he speaks Japanese admirably well. I no longer worry about you. You were able to study even during the war: This could happen only in America. My heart is filled with gratitude. You need not worry about us, either, because we are all well.

"Mr. Judge says he will relay our letters. This, too, makes me so happy. We had nothing special to offer Mr. Judge. So we offered him fruit from our persimmon tree, and he said it was delicious. He is a wonderful man. Mother."

On the reverse side of the first of the three sheets of my mother's letter, Mr. Judge scribbled:

"Kiyoaki-san,

"Banzai! As I write this note, I am surrounded by your mother and father, Akiko, Masako, Kazushige, and little Sonoko (Akiko's baby girl—& is she howling!). I have given them your letters and your pictures and they were thrilled to get them!

"I have also seen many pictures of you (for instance, one in which you are holding a little bear) and from where I sit, I can see the little 'Bull Dog' wagon in which you used to ride. I am enjoying myself tremendously, and shall write you at length as soon as I return to my headquarters. Now I must leave to take the 6:18 back to Kakogawa. Sayonara. Paul Patrick Judge."

In his November 27 letter to me, Mr. Judge reported in detail on his trip. After describing the dramatic meeting with my family, he commented: "Well, it was heavenly. To bring happiness to others is the best thing in life, isn't it?"

During the fall semester of 1945 I became more involved with the city of Northfield than before. In October, as Mr. Judge was making his way toward Kawai Mura, I was asked to address a meeting of a young people's group at the church. Before the highly attentive audience I talked about Japan and my experiences there. A few days later, Professor Alfred J. Hyslop, whose art history course I took, said to me, "You have a great influence on young people."

He explained that his teenage son had begun eating rice since hearing my talk, in which I had said that rice was the staple food of the Japanese, and that I myself used to eat four bowls for breakfast, five bowls for lunch, and six for supper.

On December 13, Thursday, the Rotary Club of Northfield invited foreign students at Carleton to a luncheon. The invitation was extended to the Cosmopolitan Club, which comprised foreign students on the campus. We were led to the luncheon by Professor David Bryn-Jones of international relations, the club's advisor. After lunch, we were asked to speak three minutes each, starting out with "Merry Christmas and a happy New Year" in our own respective languages.

As a student in Professor Bryn-Jones's class, I had usually expressed views that disagreed with his concerning Japan's foreign policy. At this Rotary luncheon, however, I felt the professor was rather proud of having me in the group.

"I am sure you would be interested to know that we have here a student from Japan," he addressed the Rotarians.

I told my audience that during the four years I had spent in the United States, I had never had an unpleasant experience on a personal basis. "I have enjoyed every minute of my life in America," I said truthfully.

In the rest of the three minutes, I mentioned what little I knew about the Rotary Clubs in Japan. I said either they were dissolved or they changed their names in 1940 under pressure from the military. But now that the war was over, I suggested, they would probably resume their activities.

This drew particularly vigorous applause from the audience. About thirty-five years later in Japan I had occasion to find out exactly what happened to the Rotary Club in Japan before the war. In the early 1940s, the military in Japan was doing its best to generate popular sentiments against the Western powers, the United States and Britain in particular. Sending officers to secondary schools and colleges to lecture on the "national crisis" confronting the country was one of the means of infusing anti-West feelings in the students. In such a Japan, the Rotary Club was viewed as a group of subversives—spies for foreign powers. To avoid the suspicion, the club disaffiliated from Rotary International in September 1940 but continued to hold its Wednesday luncheon in Tokyo as the "Wednesday Club." On March 29, 1946, it rejoined the international organization as a Rotary Club. So the guesses I made in Northfield in 1945 turned out to be essentially correct.

After the luncheon, we all shook hands with our hosts. The president was brimming with goodwill when my turn came. "I am so glad to have met you," he said, smiling. "There is nothing different about shaking hands with a Jap." Indeed, this must have been a great discovery for him.

By February 1946, when the first term of the 1945 school year ended, I had accumulated 124 credit hours, the minimum required for receiving a Bachelor of Arts degree from the college—with a major in political science. It had taken me two years and seven months since I began my freshman work at the Central YMCA College in June 1943. The strenuous thirty-one months included three summers of coursework at the YMCA College and the University of Chicago. At Carleton I carried eighteen credit hours during the first semester and twenty-three in the second, a considerably heavier load than the average of sixteen. It was hard work, especially with my part-time jobs, but I was committed to finishing my degree as soon as possible in order to fulfill my duty as a Japanese subject to serve in the military forces of Japan.

During my last semester at Carleton, however, something of radical importance dawned on me as I perused the terms of the Potsdam Proclamation Japan had accepted in surrendering to the Allied Powers. One of the conditions was: "The Japanese military forces, after being completely disarmed, shall be permitted to return to their homes with the opportunity to lead peaceful and productive lives."

As I pondered this provision, I gained a staggering realization. If all members of the Army and Navy were to be demobilized, there would be no armed forces—no Army I could join even if I wanted to. My sacred obligation had disappeared! I could hardly believe it. But on November 17, 1945, the government of Japan rescinded the Military Service Law, pursuant to the terms of the Potsdam Proclamation. I felt like an arrow that had suddenly been removed from a fully drawn bow.

At this point, I decided to stay in the United States longer than I had initially intended—to aim for a Ph.D., if possible. I wanted to continue my studies of political science as long as I could, especially since the war had provided me with a unique political perspective. The University of Chicago had an excellent political science graduate program, and furthermore it was possible there to skip an M.A. and work straight toward a Ph.D. To return home with a "doctor's degree" would be the crowning victory for a country boy who had left Japan in mid-1941, not knowing he was walking into a war that would envelop the two nations.

But there was one problem in my ambitious plan: money. When Aunt Kané had agreed to be my guarantor, both she and I myself assumed it was only for a four-year program. Now that I was aiming for a higher degree, I felt I should not count on my great-aunt's support.

The spring quarter at the University of Chicago was to begin on March 25. Rather than waiting for the June commencement at

Carleton and entering the graduate program in the fall, I decided to begin at Chicago as soon as possible. I had to earn as much as I could during the intervening seven weeks. First, I planned to find a job in Northfield. When I discussed my plan with Dr. Weigert, whose political science course I was taking in my final semester, he was very sympathetic and offered me room and board at his own home in Northfield. There was a special reason for this. In the autumn of 1945, Dr. Weigert lost his wife in a traffic accident and he was grief-stricken. He welcomed the thought of my staying with him and his two young children.

On February 3, 1946, I moved into his home. Dr. Weigert's children, Karin, about twelve, and Martin, about seven, gave me a hearty welcome as an addition to their motherless family. I played with the blond boy by tossing him toward the ceiling and he liked bouncing on the bed like a trampoline so much that he kept asking, "Once more!" almost indefinitely until I was exhausted and Dr. Weigert intervened. He reminded me of my younger brother at home because of the closeness of their ages.

That night, I dreamed that I was back at my old middle school. Unlike my dreams of the same kind in 1941, in which I was still a student, this time I was visiting my alma mater following Japan's surrender. I was in a more relaxed frame of mind, no longer concerned about military training. On the bulletin board was posted a list of the alumni of the school who were killed in action. Among my classmates there were three names. Tears rolled down my cheeks as I recognized them clearly. Somewhere on the campus, I met Mr. Kamio, the teacher of kendo and military training. I asked him, "Did you not feel like committing suicide when the war ended?" He replied, "No, not quite . . ."

I searched for a job in Northfield for three weeks. I even visited a creamery where the cans of Carnation milk that were familiar to me from my childhood were produced. But everywhere I was told that all available positions were reserved for returning veterans. Finally, I came to the belated realization that I was wasting my time trying to find a job in a small town where the newspaper carried no "help wanted" ads. On February 28, 1946, I bade farewell to the Weigerts and to the friendly little town to move to Chicago.

Chicago Again

At the University of Chicago, the student employment service directed me to the Quadrangle Club, a town-and-gown establishment on the fringes of the campus. There I found a job as a dishwasher at sixty cents an hour. After the spring term began in mid-March, I was shifted to the dining room to wait on tables for lunch and dinner—working altogether about five hours a day, seven days a week. Thus I was able to earn about $90 a month and two meals a day. Since the tuition for one quarter was $140, I had a good prospect of being able to pay for my own education.

Financial assistance also came from the International House on Fifty-ninth Street, where I had applied for and received a scholarship of $40 for a quarter for help in renting a $74 single room.

One day in March, as I was walking on campus, I saw Jerome Wodinsky again. Despite his request that we keep in touch, we had not seen each other since that summer day in August when I had met him and his ASTP friends.

"Our class is moving," he explained when I hailed him. "They are shipping us to Japan pretty soon."

A few days later I invited him to a dinner in a Japanese restaurant on the North Side with the improbable name of Delaware Garden. Jerome was excited about the prospect of going to Japan.

"I have to buy a lot of candies tomorrow before packing," he said casually.

"Candies? What for?"

"For children."

"What children? Japanese?"

"Yes. My brother is there now and he wrote to me I should bring a lot of candies because Japanese children are really crazy about them."

I was moved by his kindness and had to pause a moment before continuing to eat my sukiyaki.

At the Quadrangle Club, guests were supposed to write down their orders from the menu on checks. On one of my very first days as a waiter, I collected a check from a lone dinner guest, sitting at a small table by the walnut wall. He was chubby, fiftyish, and ruddy-faced. Because his handwriting was totally illegible, I asked the man what he had ordered. He uttered two words with a heavy European accent. The first word was incomprehensible but the second, I gathered, was "eggs." Yet there were no egg entries on the menu that night. So I asked him to repeat his order. He obliged, though he probably saw no justification for my failure to understand him except that I was new.

But the esoteric word still eluded me. I resigned myself and brought the check into the kitchen. The checker instantly deciphered the strange handwriting for me: "Shirred eggs."

It was not on the menu, but the guest ordered it every night, I was told. The kitchen accommodated him because he was a steady customer.

"And who is this man?" I asked Ed, whose job was to check the orders. "I can't read his signature, either."

"Leo Szilard. You know who he is," Ed said with a twinkle in his eyes behind thick lenses.

"You mean the atomic scientist . . . ?"

"That's right."

I recalled having read in *Life* magazine after the end of the war about the Hungarian-born scientist's role in the development of the atom bomb. He and Albert Einstein had written a letter to President Franklin D. Roosevelt, convincing him of the feasibility of using nuclear energy as a powerful weapon. And it was Szilard who demonstrated the validity of their theory by working with Enrico Fermi in the secret laboratory to produce the first controlled nuclear reaction.

While Szilard seemed to be a loner who always ate by himself at the same single table, other scientists were gregarious and lively. Among them was Edward Teller, another refugee scholar from Hungary, who was at that time probably discussing the possibility of the hydrogen bomb with his colleagues. Harold Urey, the Nobel Prize-winning chemist, who had also played a vital role in the Manhattan Project, was usually busier talking and scribbling mathematical and chemical formulae on the placemats than eating.

It seemed a historic irony that I should be waiting on these nuclear scientists who played an enormously important role in bringing the war to an end. It has been commonly held, at least in the United States, that the atom bomb saved many more human lives than it cost in that without it U.S. armed forces would have invaded Japan to force her to surrender. Such an invasion would have meant millions of casualties among Japanese civilians, who had been told and trained to use bamboo spears—for lack of any other weapon—against enemy troops.

I also noted a middleaged couple who often had their dinner at a small table by the window. The sixtyish man would have passed for an Italian farmer, by his facial features, dark skin, and English with a heavy accent. His partner, on the other hand, was a light-complexioned brunette who appeared refined, intellectual, and much younger than he. My curiosity about the seemingly incongruous pair was satisfied when I learned the man was Professor Giuseppe Antonio Borghese, a famous scholar of Italian literature and a refugee from Mussolini's Italy. The brunette was his wife Elizabeth, the youngest of Thomas Mann's daughters.

For dinner, the round table seating eight by the bay window overlooking the tennis court was reserved for a gaggle of men over sixty. It was not exclusively faculty and included some non-academic but outstanding citizens of Chicago, who represented the "town" part of the town-and-gown concept at the club. The conversation at this table was so intellectually titillating that long ago someone had thought of institutionalizing it. It was the source of the popular radio program called "The University of Chicago Round Table Discussion," aired every Sunday morning by a Chicago radio station. Waiting on this round table was a privilege to a waiter or waitress for the bits of knowledge, wisdom, and humor one could glean.

Humor at the round table could even be unintended. One evening, I heard a diner commenting on a public lecture he had recently heard on the campus, given by one Samuel I. Hayakawa. The guest was apparently very much impressed by the lecture—not so much for its substance as its delivery. He told his amazed table fellows: "By God, this Jap could speak English better than you or I."

I nearly burst out laughing. Hayakawa, a native of Canada, was a specialist in English and semantics, already famous for his *Language in Action* (1941), a popularization of Alfred Korzybsky's *Science and Sanity*. There was no reason why, despite his name and physical appearance, he should not speak English better than the average member of the Quadrangle Club.

In early December 1946, I was promoted to the position of checker because Ed was graduating soon. The new job raised my hourly wage to seventy cents from sixty-five, to which it had been raised a few months earlier.

More than that, with the new job came highly welcome perquisites. Unlike waiters and other employees, I could now punch my time card and then, while seated at the large table in the kitchen, I could eat my lunch or dinner before the rush came while checking the orders the student workers brought in and the food they took out. In retrospect, however, the most rewarding privilege I had was that I could engage in small talk with the student employees who were all my friends. I was gratified that I, a foreigner and an enemy alien until less than two years before, was supervising work by American students. Any of them would have enjoyed being in my position. But the manager chose me on the basis of the recommendation of my predecessor.

One of my duties was to maintain discipline over student workers. Jack Keller, a college student who was my junior by three or four years, and I found each other congenial even though our dispositions were poles apart. We became bosom companions, going to the movies and doing shopping together.

Occasionally, Jack would break through the invisible barrier in the kitchen to treat himself to a scoop of ice cream. Before long, the manager learned what was going on, and it became my duty to put my foot down. Not knowing this, Jack one day proceeded toward the back of the kitchen as usual when other employees were not present.

"Stop," I said.

Jack did not take me seriously because of our friendship. But friend or no friend, I had to perform my duty. To Jack's surprise, I physically intervened, as he lifted the lid of the freezer, to frustrate his ambition. But we continued to be friends.

During the first weeks of my new job, another minor problem arose. For lunch or dinner each day, the chef would put up a menu for students with a single entree. Sometimes, a student waitress would complain about a food she did not like. Having been brought up in Japan, where frugality, self-denial, and gratitude were considered virtues, I found this choosiness difficult to accept. I would chide such a complaining student half jokingly: "Haven't you read in the papers that in Europe people are eating dead horses?"

But Lorraine Leslie, one of the women students, maintained this was discrimination against students because other women employees—office staff—were allowed to choose from the day's regular menu that offered three entrees. The distinction was based on the fact that the office workers were full-time employees whereas the students were not.

I brought the matter to the manager's attention. Immediately, a meeting was convened for all concerned, including myself. The manager appeared unwilling to revise the traditional policy, insisting that the distinction between full-time and part-time employees was unavoidable under the "capitalist" system. But I argued for change, stressing a simple theme: The hardest-working employees were the students.

The meeting appeared to end inconclusively. Yet at dinnertime that day, the menu for students offered two choices instead of one. I had scored a victory for my new friends.

My correspondence with my family in Japan continued via Lieutenant Judge in Tokyo. Letters from home told of the privations that followed the surrender. The hardship was primarily due to the general deterioration of the conditions in the country. But there was also a particular factor working against our family.

Although my father was the adopted husband of the family of a landowning farmer, he could not farm because he was a schoolteacher by training. So he had to have our rice paddies tenanted by several farmers in the hamlet. The standard tenancy fee for the farmers was half of the crop yield, in return for which they paid for the costs of production. The landowner paid all property taxes.

Each year in our village, the tenant farmers would bargain collectively for a reduction in the tenancy fee. Because negotiations were between several farmers and a single landowner, the latter had a very weak position. He was the perennial underdog, and my father was a typical example.

Yet Japanese landowners like my father were one of the major targets of attack by the Allied Occupation, along with militarists and *zaibatsu*, the financial monopolies. Land reform, designed for "liberating the peasants from the yoke of landowners," therefore, was a principal aim.

The program was carried out in stages and was not completed until September 1947. But as of early 1946 the tenant farmers were allowed to pay for the use of paddies in cash, rather than by a portion of the crop. This created a serious problem for landowners in those months of food shortages and galloping inflation.

In her letter of May 6, 1946, my mother described the situation in detail. Our family received from the tenants only two *koku* (about five bushels) of rice for the crop of 1945 and, for the remainder of the harvest, cash at the rate of seventy-five yen per *koku*. The amount of rice the family received would last for only half a year, and the rice needed for the remainder of the year had to be obtained through the rationing system. What the system provided was far below the level of sufficiency, however. Most citizens who had no means of producing rice had to obtain the grain, the staple food of the nation, on the black market at exorbitant prices.

While prices in general were constantly rising, wages did not keep pace with them. My sister, who started a career as a primary school teacher after graduating from a teachers' college, was earning a monthly salary of about three hundred yen—just about sufficient to buy about a pound of beef. A pair of shoes for her would have cost one thousand yen, which she could ill afford. In early 1946, my parents decided to cultivate half an acre of rice paddy that they managed to have returned from two tenant farmers by pleading with them.

Learning these facts, I felt it was my moral duty as the eldest son of the family to do as much as I could to help.

In the autumn of 1946, I learned that relief packages could be sent from a New York shop to Japan. For $6.35, including postage, one could order a carton containing such items as powdered milk, raisins, cans of soup, and banana flakes.

Besides such commercial kits, I prepared my own parcel to send home. This was to be entrusted with Toshiko Shiraki, one of my former pupils in the advanced Japanese class at Poston. She had left the relocation center in 1944 to work for the Office of War Information in Washington. Now, in 1946, she had found a job in Tokyo with GHQ, Supreme Commander for the Allied Powers, as a DAC (Department of the Army Civilian). My plan was to ask her to take a carton to Tokyo and then mail it to my parents.

The top priority item in the package was a pair of shoes for my sister, whose size I did my level best to guess. There were six tennis balls I had picked up for my brother from among the ones discarded by Quadrangle Club members, bars of soap, cans of meat, and everything I could find to send.

Toshiko arrived in Tokyo on December 27, 1946, after a sea journey halfway around the globe from New York to Yokohama via the Panama Canal and Okinawa. This I learned from Lieutenant Judge, who had been impatiently waiting for her in Tokyo because I had informed him that one of my prize pupils was on her way.

Now I had both a former teacher and a former pupil in Japan's capital, who were willing to serve as a relay station for me and my family. In February 1947, I received a letter from Toshiko. On the last page of the five-page missive, she wrote:

> Last but not least, and with a certain amount of embarrassed hesitation, I request you send me many things. I can use foodstuffs, canned and otherwise (really, I'm always hungry!) and bar soaps are unobtainable even at the PX—I mean laundry soap. There are yards of silks and rayon but no woolens, so please oblige. Medicine of all kinds appears to be very scarce. Ever since my arrival in Tokyo, I've been having trouble with my eyes, and since I couldn't find any type of eye medicine here, I finally had to go to the 49th General Hospital. As for clothes, I shall entrust it to your excellent taste. The stock here at the PX is as limited in style as it is in quantity. And if you send anything else you think I may appreciate, I certainly shall not refuse it!

I was incredulous. Was this how the U.S. Army treated its civilian employees? After a few moments, however, I realized that this was a very clever trick Toshiko was playing on my behalf.

I had discovered in Chicago that there was a limit to the number and weight of parcel posts that could be sent to a DAC in Japan, namely, one weighing not more than eleven pounds per week. If, however, a sender presented at the post office a letter requesting shipment from home, the ceiling could be raised to seventy pounds per week. Accordingly, I had written Toshiko to send me such a letter. Her faking was so convincing I had almost believed her myself.

The envelope also contained a letter from my mother, describing in detail a visit Toshiko and Lieutenant Judge had made to Kawai Mura on February 7. Toshiko carried with her the package I had entrusted her with, besides her own presents. My mother wrote about a delightful scene of the American Army officer playing catch with Kazushige. The only sad note in her otherwise glowing letter was the fact that the shoes I had bought at Marshall Field were too small for Masako, though just right for my mother. The irony was that my mother usually wore kimono and had no use for American-made shoes.

My co-workers at the club were keenly interested in the situation in Japan and when they learned of my relief operation, they contributed many items, such as shoes and clothes for my sister. When I wanted to buy things for women at Marshall Field's, Lorraine would accompany me to do the talking with female salespeople, saving me embarrassment. At the department store I purchased a baseball glove and a baseball for Kazushige. He had also requested a dodge ball, which I found was priced at nine dollars, which I could not afford.

But I had an inspiration. I wrote to my former roommate at Carleton, Larry Gruman, now a senior, recalling that many discarded basketballs were collecting dust in a corner of the college gymnasium. Larry promptly deflated four of them and mailed them to me, along with two used baseballs.

These presents from Northfield, besides my own purchases for my brother, filled a carton. One more contained shoes donated by Lorraine and Valerie, another worker at the club, and toys sent from Lorraine's brother in Gloucester, Massachusetts.

During those months, I barely had the time to make the purchases and pack the cartons, though, because I was spending thirty-five hours in physical labor each week in addition to taking courses on an accelerated program to earn the Ph.D. After about ten months of travail, I finally realized that I was tilting at a windmill like Cervantes' hero. Meanwhile, I continued to receive letters from home, describing the difficult life my parents were leading. To them, the only bright hope was their son in America—working and studying in good health and high spirits. The thought of at least one member of the family not starving gave them encouragement and a sense of gratitude.

But my parents faced another problem. My younger sister, now nearing twenty, was already getting old for marriage by Japanese standards of the time. Yet in Japan the marriage of a daughter meant a considerable drain on her father's finances, because of the requirement of trousseaus and a dowry. The financial condition of our family made decent preparations seem impossible. The best my father could do would be in sad contrast to the affluence the newly rich farmers in the village were flaunting. But if I returned home to earn an income, it might be another story.

I knew my struggling for a Ph.D. while financing myself might take me years. By the time I returned home, my sister would be an old maid. I realized that I had to go back as soon as possible, even with only an M.A. It was a heartbreaking decision.

One person who tried to assuage my agony was Mr. Frank Mayer-Oakes, a recently demobilized naval intelligence officer who was resuming his doctorate work at the university in Japanese history. I came to know him well because he also lived at the International House. (He later became a professor at Wayne State University in Detroit.) Having studied in Japan before the war and been familiar with conditions there, he said it would be sensible for me not to spend too many years trying to earn a Ph.D. His reasoning was that an American Ph.D. would be, after all, a foreign degree in Japan, which would not receive the credit it was worth.

I accepted his avuncular counsel and decided in January 1947 to get an M.A. in political science by the end of March, exactly one year after I had started my graduate studies.

Most students would have to spend one year earning the required credits from class work and then spend another year writing a thesis, or spreading both over a two-year period.

The thesis subject of my choice was the land reform program being carried out in Japan under the Occupation, on which I had some personal knowledge because our family was being directly affected by it. The stringent task I had imposed on myself called for renewed effort to produce a thesis before the end of February. At the same time, I had to economize as much as possible to save money for my passage home. Thus, I spent about twenty-five cents for the simplest form of breakfast in the cafeteria of the International House, counting on lunch and dinner at the Quadrangle Club for nourishment. Being part of the kitchen staff, I was privileged to receive an extra dish or two of leftover dessert. As far as caloric intake was concerned, I had nothing to worry about—as long as my health held up.

After bringing my weary body back to the International House around nine o'clock at night or even later, I would head straight for my room, giving side glances at the other foreign students—mostly from Latin America—having a merry time in the lounge, playing cards or the piano. None of them seemed to need to do any work to finance their education. Whenever I had an extra hour of leisure, I would spend it taking a nap to conserve energy. The only form of recreation I indulged in was going to the movies, usually with Jack. Those two months turned out to be the most excruciating trial of my life in America.

I finished my thesis at 5:00 A.M. on March 1, 1947. But my professors told me, to my dismay, that what I had produced was only the first draft, requiring editing and improvements. Mr. Mayer-Oakes was good enough to help with the task, considerably shortening it. On his advice, I decided to aim for the June commencement rather than the one in March.

My oral examination after submission of the thesis was scheduled for May 22, a Thursday. The examiners were Professors Finer, Hardin, and Leiserson. Although the final exam was meant to give a degree candidate a chance to defend his dissertation, the questions asked of me hardly dealt with land reform in Japan at all. Instead, considerable time was spent on the new Japanese Constitution, which, promulgated on November 3, 1946, had gone into effect only three weeks before—on May 3, 1947.

While fielding the questions I had not anticipated as best I could, I worried about the possibility of flunking. If I did, all the struggle of fifteen months would have been in vain. The mental stress I felt reminded me of the session I had with the FBI agents three years earlier. That the questions ended after little more than an hour, whereas two hours were set aside for an oral, did not lessen my apprehension. How was this to be construed? Did the professors decide not to waste any more time with me because I was an obvious failure? Instead of dismissing me outright, did they go through the ritual of taking some interest in Japan—out of pity for me?

I was told to wait outside. The mounting tension was killing me, my heart beating as though I had just sprinted for two hundred yards. I was feeling weak in a way I had never felt before in my life, and almost wanted to collapse against the wall by the door of the room where such a cruel fate awaited me.

It must have been no more than three minutes, though it felt like an eon. The door opened and I saw Professor Leiserson's smiling face.

"Come in," he said.

The moment I entered, Professor Hardin said, "Congratulations!"

And then Professor Finer: "Congratulations, M.A.!"

Surprisingly, I felt no real sense of elation. Only a weighty impression that it was over, at long last, descended on me.

The commencement exercises were scheduled for June 13. Dressed in cap and gown, I sat in the Rockefeller Memorial Chapel as the pipe organ signaled the beginning of the ceremony. It was six years ago almost to the day, I realized, that I had left Japan aboard NYK's *Kamakura Maru* under ominously cloudy skies.

During those six years, I had experienced and learned so much—about the language that had seemed so formidable at first, the country called America, with which my own came to wage a disastrous war, the torrid sands of the Mojave Desert, the grillings by the FBI, the sub-zero winters of Minnesota. . . .

Throughout those months and years, I had always been mindful of the duty I had assigned myself—to study while working as much as possible—to strengthen myself with adversity. Had I lived up to my expectations?

Looking back—in the university chapel—I felt I could say to myself: "You have done better than anyone might have expected." Yet as far as adversity was concerned, I had actually experienced very little of it. True, I was always either working or studying, with movies as my sole form of relaxation. But my experience appeared incongruous with words like adversity or hardship. In retrospect, everything seemed like it had been easy and even fun. Even the chores at the Fairway Sanitarium, dismal as the environment was, appeared precious now that they were receding in my memory. The FBI? It, too, had been fun in its own way. I felt I had come out a winner because I was not, after all, incarcerated and I had been able to continue on my path.

Through all these kaleidoscopic fragments of memories, I saw a great deal of sweat, yes, but no blood or tears. This was because I had always had friends around me. Yes, I was an "enemy"—an enemy alien to the United States—but I had always been surrounded by friends.

Yet it had still been a perilous journey, because the smallest setback could have wrecked it. It could have been an illness, detention by the United States government, or just running out of steam. All in all, I have been very lucky, I told myself. What I had done was something that happened only because of a fortuitous combination of a number of factors. I knew I could not recommend what I had done to anyone else. Full of these thoughts, I could not hold back the tears rolling down my cheeks.

Chapter
16

The Long Wait

Having completed my studies in the United States, I tried to come up with a plan to return to Japan. I was also concerned about finding a job at home. Then, one of my colleagues at the club told me that the United States Army was recruiting interpreters to work in the International Military Tribunal in Tokyo. He had seen a notice on the bulletin board at Cobb Hall, the administration building.

I could go home without spending a cent! And I'd have a job in hand. I immediately filed an application with the Civil Service Commission. There was a language test conducted by two examiners, an American and a middleaged Japanese. They gave me the highest mark, making me feel my policy of learning English words and phrases along with their Japanese counterparts had paid off.

Soon I received a notice from the Department of the Army giving me a "tentative appointment" with a pay grade of GS-8 in the sixteen-tier scale for civil servants. The monthly salary in dollars that seemed fabulous would, I felt, certainly enable me to support my family in the country while I worked in Tokyo. Getting my sister married off with decent preparations would be a cinch. The looming possibilities seemed almost too good to be true.

On July 15, I reported for a physical held at the Fifth Army Headquarters and received many inoculation shots. On that day I also received several pamphlets, giving useful information about going to Japan. One of them said that the Military Air Transport Service (MATS) plane to carry me across the Pacific had only bucket seats and that passengers should not expect the same comfort available on a commercial liner. It did not matter. I was flying home! It meant a vast difference from the sea voyage that would take two weeks between San Francisco and Yokohama. I felt I was now very close to home.

But the Army could not tell me exactly when I would be flying to Japan, except that it would not be before the beginning of September. For the first time in America, I found myself with leisure time on hand. So, I took a two-week tour of the East—from Washington to Boston and Buffalo.

After my return to Chicago, weeks passed but no instructions on my departure for Tokyo came. In late November, I telephoned the Fifth Army Headquarters and learned it had no information about the matter. Only the Department of the Army in Washington, I was told, would be able to resolve my problem.

In early December, I took a train ride to Washington—for the second time in four months. My destination was the Pentagon.

Still quite new at the time—it had been completed in early 1943—the world's largest office building was already famous for its labyrinthine features. I knew that my errand would not be accomplished very quickly if only because of the design of the building. Besides, how would I find the right man to answer my questions?

My initial approach was to the information desk of the Department of the Army. My question was no doubt a tough one: I have a tentative appointment as a GS-8 to work in the International Military Tribunal, Far East, in Tokyo. I would like to know when I am supposed to leave.

The information clerk had to think for a moment. Finally, she gave me directions to an office that "might be able to help" me. There, I repeated my question and then it was suggested I try another office. This process was repeated several times. In the meantime, walking half a mile, climbing stairways and turning several corners at obtuse angles, I completely lost my bearings, as do most first-time visitors to the Pentagon.

At long last, however, I found myself at the bull's eye. The man in mufti did not have to direct me to another office because he *had* the answer. He must have been the official concerned with the recruitment of Japanese-English interpreters for the war crimes trials in Tokyo.

"Your tentative appointment was cancelled," he said flatly.

"Why?"

"It's not our policy to give out the reasons."

"Why wasn't I informed of it?"

"We sent you a letter, but it was returned because you were not at the address," he said, looking at the letter he had fished out of a file. It was sent in early August, I was told, which was shortly after I had left Chicago on my trip. I had wasted nearly four months! My only consolation was that the vain waiting had given me a chance to travel through the East.

But why the cancellation? As I made my way out of the building, I pondered over the reasons. Had I been rejected on the basis of citizenship? When I initially applied for the job, I was simply told to fill out a form for civil service. My nationality and allegiance were not asked. Apparently, there was the assumption that anyone applying for a civil service job was a citizen of the United States. But if this was the case, had my examiners not noticed that I was not an American citizen?

Or perhaps citizenship was not a requirement, but when my case was checked after the tentative appointment, it was discovered that I was still technically an enemy alien, not even an alien with permanent residence. And furthermore, if an inquiry had been made with the FBI, my dossier would have been offered, with the notation of "pending" on the last sheet of the report by Agent Orton. Despite my disappointment, I felt a secret pride at the notion that my status as an enemy alien had not been discovered until the FBI file had appeared.

In any event, I now knew where I stood with the Department of the Army. I immediately applied for an exit permit with the Department of State to go back to Japan on my own. But this also meant a wait of several months, I was told, because the issuance of a permit was contingent upon approval by General MacArthur's headquarters in Tokyo.

"Why do I need a permit to return to my own country?" I wondered. It did not take me long to find the answer. Articles in newspapers about the Allied Occupation of Japan made it clear to me that GHQ, SCAP, would not like to have even Japanese citizens enter the country if they were to prove to be inimical to the purpose of the Occupation, namely, the democratization of Japan.

In late January 1948, six months after my graduation, as I worked in maintenance at the Quadrangle Club, I received an order from the Chicago office of the Immigration and Naturalization service to present myself there.

As I faced the dour-looking official, I was asked a question I had fully anticipated: You came into the United States as a student and completed your studies. Why are you still here?

"Why am I still here?" indeed. I felt I should be the one to ask the government that question. I should have been back in Japan long before. I had been allowed to enter the United States "solely for the purpose of study." It meant that as soon as I completed my education in school, I was required to return to Japan. I seemed to be dawdling, but not because I wanted to. I explained what had happened with the Army and that now I had to wait for an exit permit from the Department of State.

"I would be happy if you would deport me," I said, naively thinking that deportation was the most expeditious way of traveling to Japan and at Uncle Sam's expense to boot.

"No, we wouldn't like to deport you," the official said. "If you were deported, you wouldn't be able to return to the United States." Then, to my surprise, he added casually, "We would like you to come back here."

"Then, I wish you would tell the Department of State to hurry up and process my application."

The official managed to suppress a smile and said, "We don't advise a brother service about what they are doing. We'll wait. Don't worry. You do what you have been doing."

It took the State Department four months to issue me an exit permit, which came in early April 1948. I had been waiting nearly a year. Fortunately, I had managed to save some money for my passage home in the interim, and the added months of relative leisure had given me the opportunity to socialize with my colleagues at the Quadrangle Club. I packed my belongings and was ready to leave Chicago for San Francisco to catch a ship leaving for the Far East on April 24.

A few days before my planned departure, Chris Collins, one of the student workers at the club, said to me, "Kiyo, will you go to Michelle's apartment at 8:30 tonight? She has something to show you." He had a smile on his face that puzzled me. Michelle Furness was a college student from Boston, where her father was a wealthy businessman. Michelle, who "hated capitalists," was a self-proclaimed socialist. She and Chris, who probably shared the same ideology, were close friends. They had apartments in the same building not far from campus. But why should he tell me to visit her at night? Though mystified, I agreed.

During the afternoon, I went to the Central Camera Shop on South Wabash Avenue downtown to pick up some prints of pictures I had taken. The ban on enemy aliens possessing contraband had been lifted in late 1947, and I had purchased a recently marketed 35-mm camera called a Bolsey. I had taken many shots of my friends, and I wanted to give them the prints as souvenirs.

While I was in the shop, John Mellinger, another student worker, came in and seemed surprised to find me there. He told me he was thinking of learning how to develop photos, and began examining developing tanks for 35-mm film.

"Which would you choose, Kiyo, if you were to buy one—Bakelite or stainless steel?"

"I would prefer a stainless steel one. Bakelite breaks and chips easily," I said knowingly, borrowing expertise from a camera buff friend.

"By the way, do you plan to develop your own pictures when you go back to Japan?"

"I haven't thought about it. But now that you mention it, I might try."

John purchased the stainless steel tank, a yellow filter, and a filter holder. He then wanted to see if the holder fit the Bolsey I had. He then looked at some books on photography and bought one on filters and another on tank developing.

That night, I knocked on the door of Michelle's apartment punctually at 8:30 P.M. We chatted briefly about my schedule for returning to Japan and related subjects. But soon we ran out of topics. What was more, I found Michelle ill at ease. She had wanted to see me, according to Chris, and she did appear to have expected me. Yet she seemed awkward; occasionally she would leave her room to walk down the hall and then come back. As minutes went by, the atmosphere became even more awkward. But she did not seem to want me to leave.

About nine o'clock, she went out again and said when she returned: "Kiyo, I want you to come to Chris's room. I have something to show you."

Wrapped in suspense, I followed her down the hall. When I opened the door, the mystery evaporated. I found all of my fellow student workers from the Quadrangle Club there—Dorothy, Claire, Shirley, Lorraine, Arthur, Charles, the two Bills, Bob, John, and, of course, Jack—filling the small room. They greeted me with a mirthful cry of "Surprise!" On the table were cans of beer and soft drinks, and bowls of pretzels.

"So this is what you have been scheming behind my back."

They toasted my safe homeward voyage.

As if to represent the group, Michelle picked up a parcel from the mantelpiece. "This is a little something from us."

When I opened it, there was the second surprise of the evening. It contained the camera equipment and books I had helped John acquire during the afternoon.

Then came a spontaneous chorus:

> For Kiyo is a jolly good fellow;
> For Kiyo is a jolly good fellow;
> For Kiyo is a jolly good fellow;
> Which nobody can deny,
> Which nobody can deny . . .

My heart was full. It was hardly necessary for me to make a speech because everyone knew how I felt. Yet I wanted to say something. "You have been a wonderful bunch," I managed. "I really enjoyed working with you at the club for the last two years. I was able to accomplish my purpose because of you.

"But I was completely fooled by your conspiracy today."

John said, "You knew I was buying the filter for your camera this afternoon, didn't you?"

"Hell no," I said. "I thought you, too, had a 35-mm camera. Why should I think you were buying the filter for me? I had no idea of why I was supposed to come to Michelle's apartment, either."

When the day came for me to leave Chicago, Jack was to take me to Northwest Station in his old Ford, because he was the only one who had a car. That afternoon, I heard a honk in Brent House, my temporary abode, and went out to the sidewalk on Woodlawn Avenue with two suitcases. The car was filled with my friends, who also wanted to see me off at the station.

"This is my present," Jack said, shoving a folded chessboard and a box of chessmen at me.

"For heaven's sake," I whimpered, "there is not a cubic inch of space in my suitcase."

Jack was unconcerned. "We are going to play an international chess match by air mail, aren't we, Kiyo, giving our moves one at a time?"

"We did talk about that, Jack, but . . ."

Jack would not take no for an answer.

At the station, I made certain that the eighteen pieces of luggage for the ship's hold were there to be loaded on the *City of San Francisco*. My friends came to the train side to bid me farewell. I sat down in my seat after the deluxe streamliner started to move—with the chess set on my lap. As I saw the lights flit by with increasing speed, I looked back on my Chicago days—from that May Sunday of 1943 when I was greeted by the little girl in Grant Park, the steamy summer days of 1945 when the bloody war ended, and the months of hardship through my graduate studies, working with splendid friends. They had been with me until a few minutes ago and I might never see them again.

Luckily, the seat next to me was vacant so I let the tears roll down my cheeks freely.

Chapter
17

A Man with No Name

Back in San Francisco after seven years, I visited Drew School first. Although the wooden school building looked hardly different on the outside, Mr. Drew had retired and many of the teachers I had known there were no longer there. Among them, of course, was Mr. Judge.

I also called on Mr. Judge's mother. She introduced me to Mr. Judge's younger sister, who was working as a district attorney. In her office, I asked her about her work. She said, "Never a dull moment"—a phrase I found quite interesting—and gave me a few details. I also met Mr. Judge's sister-in-law and her young son, with whom I struck up a good relationship. When I was about to leave, the baby began to cry, which I took as a compliment.

Another person I looked up was Susumu Takao, Mrs. Shimizu's brother. He had remained in Poston until the end of the war and was now back in San Francisco, working at the Post Office. We talked mostly about what had happened to the others in the intervening years. Since my release from the camp, Mr. Shimizu had been transferred to Poston from the detention center, and the Shimizus and Aunt Kané had moved to Cincinnati. Aunt Kané sold the San Leandro nursery to the florist who had been renting it during the war years. With the capital from the sale, they began a business in beansprout production, which proved successful.

Other evacuees had not been so lucky. At Poston we had heard of some families that had been forced to sell their property at a loss because of the evacuation. In recent years I have read accounts of property "confiscated," though I did not hear of such occurrences at any time during the war.

On the other hand, Susumu and I had heard many Nisei saying, "One good thing that came out of the war is that we rediscovered America by living in areas other than the West Coast, thanks to the evacuation." I had heard of a Nisei who migrated to the East Coast and became a member of an exclusive country club. One day, he brought a *hakujin* friend to the club. Later he was told: "You are welcome here, but don't bring Jews here again."

The ship on which I had booked passage home was the *General Meigs*, a former transport ship American President Lines leased from the government to carry passengers across the Pacific. Essentially a freighter, the ship had a simple design, with one flat deck, a few cabins (euphemistically called staterooms), and a large hold for accommodating thousands of passengers on as many bunks.

When I bought a ticket in Chicago, I was told not to have illusions about the "stateroom," which accommodated the first-class passengers. As it turned out, it was a cabin with twelve steel beds on three tiers. This was where officers had been quartered during the war while the cavernous hold below carried enlisted men. The war being over less than three years, all the stenciled signs and instructions for troops on the ship remained intact.

The Pacific Ocean itself seemed unchanged since before the war, with the same greenish blue billows, through which the *General Meigs* relentlessly plowed westward. But I knew that during the years since the first time I crossed it, the sea had turned into a graveyard for hundreds of thousands of men. According to Japanese war records, the figure for Japanese dead at sea was 473,000, of whom 135,000 were civilians.

Several of the stateroom passengers were American missionaries bound for Japan—most of them returning to reopen their missions in the cities where they had worked before the war. These were my daily companions and fellow diners.

On an oceanliner each passenger came to know everyone else without an effort. Within a few days I was comfortably chatting with all the Americans—except one.

He was a young man of my age and height with dark, curly hair, a ruddy complexion, and a stoop. He spent most of the time reading alone; occasionally he would speak with a few Chinese passengers. He always wore tinted eyeglasses, as though he wanted to avoid facing other human beings. He seemed afraid and even furtive. In short, he was utterly alien to the American prototype I had come to know through my seven years of life in America. Furthermore, he appeared to be purposely avoiding me.

It was most likely that my voyage would have come to its end without my knowing anything about this man. However, on the night of May 4, four days before the ship was due to dock at Yokohama, we struck up a conversation in the company of other passengers in the lounge. While I was chatting with my Japan-bound missionary friend, the mystery man sitting nearby casually volunteered: "I have been to Japan."

I was surprised to hear him speaking to me after ten days of determined reticence. When I asked him where he was headed, he said he was going to Nanking. He was still cold to me, though no longer inaccessible. Gradually, he opened up.

One of the first things he said about himself was: "I was with military intelligence in China during the war."

In the ensuing discourse, after other passengers had left us for a game of bingo in the same lounge, I learned the remarkable facts.

During my life in wartime America, I would from time to time wonder if there had been anyone who had crossed the Pacific Ocean in the opposite direction about the time I traveled to the United States. And if there had been one, what might have happened to him—what kind of experience he might have had in Japan, particularly in contrast to mine in the United States.

This person I faced now on my homeward voyage across the Pacific said he had gone to Japan as one of six exchange students "a few months before the war broke out." I had not known there was such an arrangement for exchange students between the two countries.

When the war began, all six of the American students in Japan were placed in custody just as diplomats and other residents were. They were treated well. But then the students escaped with the help of a Chinese underground group and found their way to China. There, they were caught by the Japanese military, who accused them of having been American spies. They were tortured.

But somehow he and at least a few others escaped and went to Nanking, where they joined the OSS.

While working behind the Japanese lines as an agent, he was captured again.

"They beat me so hard that my right eardrum became perforated. I could not eat for weeks because my mouth swelled from the beatings."

During captivity he was shown one of his friends who had been subjected to even harsher treatment. "His eyes had been taken out of his head. He died shortly after. I saw him too late."

Suddenly, he pulled up his sweater to reveal a dark scar the size of a silver dollar on his right side. "They used the point of a bayonet." He paused. "I wish my tormentors had beaten me harder."

Until then, his sole purpose in life had been to help fellow human beings. He had been a medical student in Japan because he believed in human goodness. When he joined the OSS in Nanking, he had fully expected to return to his studies after the war was over.

But his captivity led to utter disillusionment. Human beings were despicable; human lives were not worth saving. He even felt he could not go on living himself. Although the physical pain went away with time, he said, the trauma to his mind never did. Life became unbearable. He could not trust other people; he constantly feared they would deceive, betray, and hurt him.

After the war, he joined military intelligence again because he wanted to be near death to seek surcease from his suffering.

His soliloquy was a meditative reminiscence, not a denunciation of dire deeds by his fellow men. He spoke so softly that some of his words were drowned out by the noise from the bingo game behind us. But details such as places, dates, and even the sequence of events seemed to matter little. What did matter was the fact that we had met at all, and the contrast in our experiences during the war years: he lost, while I gained, faith in humanity. It was a revelation.

"The last time I talked to a Japanese," he said toward the end of our conversation, "I was chained to a chair and thought I would never talk to another Japanese again. But I don't hate you, even though you are one of them."

Now his mysterious behavior made perfect sense. I was overcome with conflicting emotions. I asked him to write something in my notebook—his life's motto—and he obliged:

> So many Gods; so many creeds
> So many paths that wind and wind,
> When just the art of being kind,
> Is all this sad world needs.

By then, it was about one o'clock in the morning of May 5, and we were alone in the lounge. A cabin attendant came around to put back all the clocks by half an hour as he did every night. We had been sitting together for three hours.

Before we returned to our respective staterooms, I asked the man, "By the way, what is your name?"

He said, "Please remember me as a man with no name."

The *General Meigs* entered Japanese waters early in the morning of May 8. I knew this because the Boso Peninsula was on the horizon—the first part of the Japanese landscape to greet any westbound ship headed for Yokohama.

"So this is my fatherland again," I thought—the country that survived such furious aerial bombings. The government had surrendered unconditionally to its enemies, but the green mountains still glistened in the late spring sun.

When my ship was berthed, two noncommissioned officers of the local military government team of the Allied Occupation came aboard. Desks and chairs were set up for processing disembarking passengers. A reporter from a newspaper also came aboard for possible stories. Apparently a recently demobilized veteran, he wore an Army uniform and boots as his work clothes. His attire drove home to me the reality of life in post-surrender Japan that I had only read about in the American press.

"Are you a buyer?" asked the man from behind the desk. He was an ethnic Japanese.

"No. I am a student. I have just returned."

My answer seemed to puzzle him. There was no such classification on the list of entrants he was to process. Entry into Japan was highly restricted, and the few categories under which it was possible included "buyer," meaning a businessman to sample what Japan could hope to export to the United States. Missionary was another.

"You mean you are a repatriate?"

"I don't think so. I am a student."

It was my turn to be puzzled. A repatriate was a person returned to his home country after a war, during which he was displaced or detained. I had read about hundreds of thousands of Japanese repatriates who had returned or were still returning from other parts of Asia, such as Korea, China, and Siberia. They had been prisoners of war and civilian detainees. I was neither.

I had gone to the United States and was returning after completing my plan. But apparently, the noncommissioned officer classified me as a "repatriate," which, as it turned out, was technically correct. But I did not know it, so I did not go through the "repatriation" desk.

After disembarkation, I went to the Yokohama branch of the Bank of Japan to exchange into yen the twenty United States dollars I was allowed to bring in. At the bank, I was asked to show a repatriate's certificate, which I did not have. I was told I should obtain it from the Repatriation Assistance Agency in Tokyo.

I managed to get a ticket on the government railway train from Yokohama to Tokyo. I glanced at the other passengers in the train, and was relieved to see that people were not as unhealthy as I had imagined. At least a year or two earlier, I had read of people starving and dropping dead on the street.

The ruins testifying to devastation by air raids and the shoddy clothes people wore pained my heart. By contrast, my suit—a twenty-nine-dollar bargain for the jacket and two pants in Chicago—appeared almost elegant. Indeed, the other people on the train stared at my clothing as if they were wondering what sort of high official I was.

When I arrived at my destination in Tokyo's Kasumigaseki, I learned that the certificate of repatriation I needed could be issued only by the agency's Yokohama branch. Each time a ship arrived, the local office would prepare the paper for each of the disembarking Japanese citizens by the passenger list they received in advance.

I headed back for Yokohama to go to the repatriation office in the hills in the suburbs of the city, reached by a local train, just before five o'clock in the afternoon. The official in charge there had anticipated my coming because I was the only passenger who had not claimed the certificate on the ship.

"We were worried about you," he said, because of my failure to claim the paper aboard the ship.

"*Gokurosama*," he said to comfort me as he handed me the document. "You have nothing to worry about now." The Japanese expression is used to show appreciation of hardship undergone by someone. The official naturally assumed that I deserved sympathy for having suffered through life in hostile territory and, now that I was home, I could finally relax among my countrymen.

"No," I said inwardly. I did not deserve his compassion and comforting. I had had no "hardship" to speak of—at least nothing compared with what people at home had been through. If anyone should have said "*gokurosama*," it was I who should have said it, to the people of Japan.

At Yokohama Station I received a free ticket home by presenting the repatriation certificate. The national railway was performing its function of running all the lines. But for travel between Tokyo and Kobe and beyond, the express trains were gone. Only local trains that made all the stops were in service. It would take me fifteen hours to get home. I promptly telegraphed my parents to inform them of my arrival, just as I had said I would in my imaginary letter to Fujiwara so many years before. The train I rode had seats covered with gunnysack, and the windows were all boarded up.

Our village remained intact, sparkling in verdant glory. My father was standing near the rural road running by our house. We smiled at each other, but, again, there was no hugging or any overt expression of emotions. It was, in fact, as awkward as was our parting at Sannomiya Station in Kobe on that rainy day seven years before.

Inside the house, Mother was gleeful. But there was nothing much to talk about because we had full knowledge of each other through the letters that Mr. Judge had passed on for us. The only important matter was the confirmation that we survived the war and were together again. Inside the house was an attractive young woman I did not recognize at first. It was my younger sister, Masako, who had grown from a teenage middle school student to a schoolteacher. My brother, fifteen years my junior, was somewhat bashful toward me, a stranger.

The only missing member of the family was my great-grandmother, who had seen me off on the train in front of our house. She had died in August 1943 at the age of ninety-one.

To be sure, my plan for studies in America had been somewhat delayed by war. But I did manage to attain the goal for which I had set out when I was eighteen years old. In that sense, I did not fail one of the cardinal instructions given to every Japanese middle school student: "Persevere in your endeavor. Once you start doing something worthwhile, never give up halfway or waver in going through with it."

Epilogue

In the autumn of 1983, I was invited by Carleton College to return to receive an honorary degree. I was ecstatic about the prospect of being able to visit my alma mater after thirty-eight years. Throughout the nearly four decades, I had often thought about Carleton. Memories of the smallest details and episodes remained clear in my mind. I had hungered to return there some day, one day, not knowing how or when it would ever come. Although I had been back to the U.S. many times, I did not wish to visit the campus casually, on the way to another city, or hurriedly, during a stopover between flights. I had vainly hoped for some legitimate reason to take a separate trip. And now the dream seemed to be coming true.

My trip to Carleton was one of the most sentimental journeys of my life. As decades had elapsed since I last saw Northfield in early 1946, I sometimes wondered if the town and the college really existed—the brownstone buildings, the observatory, the chapel, and Margaret Evans Hall, where I had gained my dubious fame as a judo expert. The entire place may have disappeared, I thought, like the "vanishing village" we read about in our German language class, which appeared once every hundred years or so.

When I arrived on the campus on June 8, 1984, the old landmarks were there, but several new buildings had been added and the trees had grown larger. All I needed, I thought, was a time slip to send me on a trip along the fourth dimension to 1944—to surprise the members of the faculty and the students.

On the following day, the commencement ceremonies took place on the Bald Spot, a large grassy space that, when flooded in the Minnesota winter, turned into a natural ice-skating rink.

The citation that was read as I accepted the honorary degree was surprising as well as flattering. It referred to the article I contributed to *The Carletonian* in the spring of 1945 concerning the Japanese Emperor. I had nearly forgotten ever having written such a thing.

In my address, titled "An 'Enemy' Among Friends," I described my life in wartime America, and ended my address saying:

"From my wartime life in the United States, I learned the importance of the individual as the basic element of humanity—not a member of a category of people such as a nation or an ethnic group. I am grateful to the American people I lived and worked with during the 1940s for giving me the opportunity to learn that important philosophy of life. . . ."

Several weeks later, I received from the college a clipping of a column by Mr. John Karras in the *Des Moines Sunday Register* of June 17. It began:

"One does not expect to be bowled over by a commencement address. One expects, instead, to wander mentally among cheerful thoughts as the exhortations and clichés wash harmlessly over the psychic void.

"But this commencement address was different. This commencement address had us holding our breath. This commencement address was a compelling testament of man's humanity to man when least expected. . . ."

I began to feel uneasy. Could the columnist possibly be referring to my speech? And he was. Mr. Karras was at the Carleton commencement as the father of a graduating student.

The writer, who was eleven years old when Pearl Harbor came, recalled the virulent anti-Japanese propaganda of those years. "Everyone I knew at the time hated the Japanese," he wrote. "To 'Jap' a person was to stab him in the back, as in, 'Hey, it's okay for you to turn around. I won't Jap ya.'

"That, then, was the temper of America shortly after the young Kiyoaki Murata arrived. He did not speak of fear in his remarks at Carleton, but he must have known it. How could he not have, surrounded as he was by the high-fever ravings of wartime hatred?

"He spoke, instead, of friendship and kindness."

The truth is, Mr. Karras, I did not *avoid* mentioning fear in my remarks because I had not felt fear. I did not *choose* friendship and kindness as topics just to pretty up my speech: I was simply recounting what I had experienced. And that is exactly what I have done in this little memoir with the same title as my commencement address.